THE ✦ TIMES

choosing [your] career

Work out
WHAT YOU REALLY WANT
to do with your life

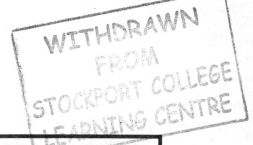

SALLY LONGSON

First published 2000
Reprinted 2000

Kogan Page Limited
120 Pentonville Road
London N1 9JN

British Library Cataloguing in Publication Data

A CIP record for this book is available from the British Library.

ISBN 0 7494 3111 3

Typeset by JS Typesetting, Wellingborough, Northants
Printed and bound in Great Britain by Clays Ltd, St Ives plc

Contents

Preface

Choosing your career doesn't mean you'll spend the rest of your life in one job. The reality is, you will – at some stage – change your career.

Some people have clearer ideas about their future career and life than others. When someone asks you what you're going to do after the course you're on now, do you:

☐ tell them about your career plans? You're sorted;
☐ waffle about your plans, trying to sound convincing? You *think* you're on the right track…;
☐ wish they'd all clear off? You don't know, and there's no need for them to remind you that you don't.

We're all different. Career choice is a very personal matter. The career that's right for your best mate won't necessarily suit you. You'll spend a lot of time at work, so it's important to find work you enjoy and find satisfying. This book will help you work out where your future might be – it has a strong focus on *you*. It'll also help you overcome any other worries you've got … most people have some; it's only natural.

Do any of these apply to you? Do you worry about:

☐ being unemployed?   _____
☐ being stuck in a dead end job without prospects?   _____
☐ being on the dole for a long time?   _____
☐ coping at work?   _____
☐ failing?   _____
☐ living up to everyone's expectations of you?   _____
☐ being in one job forever?   _____
☐ making the right choice?   _____
☐ paying off your debts?   _____

If you've ticked any of these, I hope this book will help you tackle some of your concerns. But fear is never a bad thing. It drives you forward. It keeps your eyes open and your ears to the ground; it keeps you alert for new opportunities.

This book has lots of quizzes and questions and practical exercises to help you make up a picture – or a vision – of where you're headed. They're marked like this:

 You should keep these answers together to build a picture of yourself.

To alert you to all the jobs and careers out there, I've mentioned as many as I can without going into massive detail about them. If you don't know what a sector or job involves, ask somebody, or head off to your careers library and find out. Jot down the sectors and jobs that leap out at you and make you think, *'Wait a minute – that might be for me…'* Check them out in the careers library – they might be just what you're looking for. But don't expect to decide on your career overnight – that's impossible.

FINALLY...

If you don't know what you want to do with your life, two things can happen: you do nothing about it and keep worrying or don't care; or you do something about it and move off the starting post.

I promise you, you'll feel much better if you choose the second route. So let's get started...

CHAPTER ONE

Don't know what to do?

DON'T PANIC – BUT GET THINKING

Everyone around you probably keeps telling you how important your career choice is. 'Oh God,' you cringe, when yet another person comes up to ask you about your future plans. 'I wish you'd stop asking,' you think. 'I *don't* know what I'm doing and it doesn't help when people keep going on about it.' You wish you could hide for the next few years, 'til the whole thing goes away.

Deep down, what really worries you is that you think they're right. The decision you make now will affect your lifestyle and the direction you take for the next few years. It's a major decision you have to make. It's your choice, nobody else can do it for you. But there are lots of people out there who'll happily help you to make the right choice if you give them the chance – and this book will guide you along the path to finding what you want, too.

So how are careers created? How do people get to where they are?

It's like this. You get people who can say:

- ☐ *'I know what I want to do!'*
- ☐ *'I've got a vague idea!'*
- ☐ *'I haven't got a clue!'*

People who know what they want usually set off in their late teens and twenties on their chosen path. They move from one stepping stone to another, on their journey to be whatever it is they want, until their journey is complete and they've arrived. Every stage takes effort and determination – but the fact they know where they're headed makes it all easier. They've got a goal.

Some people don't even wait to finish their formal education to start work. They find their own niche – maybe computing, singing, or writing – and sell their expertise to the public. Others have to wait a little longer for their big chance:

> I want to be an actor. My day job pays the bills while I'm waiting for my big break. I've worked as a waiter, in an office and as a children's entertainer. It gets to be very frustrating, but I'd never forgive myself if I didn't try.
>
> David, aged 36

Some of us roam around, wondering where we're headed, for much longer...

Careers lessons at school go over our heads. *'Did we really have a careers library? Where was it, then?'* We leave, spend our late teens and twenties finding out about who we are and what we want in life. We roam about, looking for a spot we like to settle in. We travel, do odd jobs, have a laugh and make the whole thing up as we go along, while our ex-school mates are forging ahead with their careers. There are loads of people sitting at their desks, doodling on a piece of paper between phone calls, thinking, *'I wonder if I could be a...?'* or *'I want to do something else. I wonder what, though?'* This can apply to the graduate at work as much as the person who left school at 16.

It's possible to retrain and start a new career. But lots of people stay in the same job, thinking, *'Oh well, at least it brings the cash in and pays for the mortgage and food bill.'* Much depends on your own 'get up and go' to make the change; careers advice and wishful thinking won't solve everything.

'Never mind the roaming round, let's just get into a job and on with life.' You also get people who've got no direction and who just take what comes their way without any ambitions. Nap time and life outside work is more important than what they're doing to bring the cash in.

> My friend Kate started with this insurance company. She was doing okay, so I asked her to find out if there were any vacancies going. And then the personnel manager rang me up and asked me to come in for an interview – they were looking for new staff, and Kate had told her a bit about me. And the next thing I knew, I was starting work.
>
> Martin, insurance company

> I never planned my career. I just fell into jobs as they came along. I concentrated on doing the things I was doing very well – and then the openings just seemed to open up, so I'd move into them. But I never actually sat down and said to myself, this is where I want to be in 10 years' time or whatever. I often wonder where I'd be if I *had*.
>
> Suki, office manager

AND THEN, THERE'S YOU. LET'S GET A GRIP ON YOUR CAREER PLANNING SO FAR.
(And don't worry if you haven't done any. This book's here to help you do some.)

Seriously, can you write down:

☐ the broad area you'd like to work in, eg engineering, design, caring, health, leisure, etc?
☐ the sort of job you'd like to do?

- [ ] the people you'd like to be working with?
- [ ] where you'd want to work?
- [ ] how work would fit in with your lifestyle?

Don't panic if you have no clue what comes next in your life – as we've seen from the above examples, lots of people didn't really know what they wanted when they left full-time education, either. This book will help you get a jump-start over them, and get a focus and a grip on your future.

Challenge Yourself!

Accept that you're not sure what you want to do. Don't waste time and energy worrying about it. Do something about it.

'But I'm so busy – I just don't seem to have time!'

Careers planning is all too often forgotten in the effort to complete your coursework, prepare for exams, go out with friends, work part-time, follow hobbies and interests... But remember that:

- [ ] everything you do is building up your skills base for the future and teaching you how to balance your home life and work;
- [ ] if you can focus on what you want out of life, you can focus on what you need to do to work towards it;
- [ ] you can always make time, if you manage your life wisely – for example, you can do careers planning during the holidays as much as during term time;
- [ ] the Internet is a mine of careers information – no longer are you restricted to getting to the careers library before 5.30 pm.

The key is to treat your career with the seriousness it deserves. Make your career planning a priority. Don't fret, take action.

Plus, if you're worried about debt and money, make an appointment and talk to your bank or building society. After all, you'll need money to:

☐ apply for jobs – you'll need stationery, postage and the use of a telephone;
☐ make sure you're appropriately dressed for interviews.

The bank or building society who sees that you're making a serious attempt to get a job and move your career forward will want to help you.

'But what if I make the wrong decision, though?'

top T I P

To reduce the risk of making a wrong decision about your career and life, you need to take action and do your homework. Find out about yourself and build up a solid picture of the workplace.

Get serious about making decisions!

Get a feel for how and why you make decisions – it will help you understand what's involved in deciding the way forward. Let's look at your current strategies for making any decisions – what to wear, where to go on a Saturday night, what to do at the weekend, etc.

 How do you make decisions?

☐ By instinct?
☐ By finding out as much as you can about the options?
☐ By just going for the one which is the least hassle?
☐ By getting others to tell you what to do?
☐ By doing it last minute – it can be an excuse if things go wrong?
☐ By weighing up the pros and cons?

☐   By thinking about what is right for you?
☐   By looking at the whole picture?
☐   By pleasing others?

What does this tell you about the way you choose to do things?

| Q | **Is anything stopping you from making decisions about your career?** |

	YES	NO
☐ Fear of making the wrong decision?	___	___
☐ Worry over what other people will think?	___	___
☐ Fear of change?	___	___
☐ Can't find the time to do it?	___	___
☐ Don't know where the careers library is, or who the careers adviser is?	___	___
☐ Niggling worries starting with *'What if?'*	___	___
☐ Not knowing where to start ... the whole situation just seems too enormous to handle?	___	___
☐ Other	___	___

WORK IT OUT

To make a good, sound decision you need to:

■   do proper research and make full use of the resources available to you.

■   share your thoughts with people who know you – see what they think.

■   allow time to find things out and think about your career and your life.

■   get to know the whole picture and where you fit.

How thorough were you *really* when you chose the course you're studying now?

| Q | When you chose your current course, did you: |

		YES	NO
☐	Talk to *all* your subject teachers about your potential?	___	___
☐	Talk to employers about future opportunities?	___	___
☐	Read books about choosing a career?	___	___
☐	Talk to your parent(s) about your choices?	___	___
☐	Think carefully about what you might be good at?	___	___
☐	And discuss it with friends and family?	___	___
☐	Listen carefully to career talks (be honest)?	___	___
☐	Attend careers conventions and ask questions?	___	___
☐	Think about the workplace and what you might do in it?	___	___
☐	Talk to students currently studying the courses you were considering applying for, so that you could find out what they were like?	___	___
☐	Take part in opportunities to learn about the workplace?	___	___
☐	Check the Internet for careers information?	___	___
☐	Talk to people at work about what they do?	___	___
☐	Get work experience?	___	___

The more wholeheartedly you can do the above, the more likely you are to make an informed career choice!

If you ticked yes:

10+   You really researched your career options well.

7–9   You put some effort into checking out your choices – but not much. Was it lack of time, interest or your own organization?

4–6   You weren't taking all this seriously, were you?

0–3   Get with it! This is *your* life we're talking about!

What did your method of choosing your present course teach you about:

☐   the importance you placed on your career at the time – do you see it differently now?

☐   how you make decisions?

☐   listening to people?

☐   who you trust for advice?

'But does career planning really matter? What about those people who didn't know what they were going to do, that you mentioned at the start of this chapter? They've done okay, haven't they?'

Things have changed since they left school, at work and in education. If you've never seriously thought about your career, here's...

| 6 | reasons to work out what you want... |

1.   Life is much more fun when you're doing the things you *want* to do and you're doing things you're good at.

2.   You'll waste time doing jobs you don't want to do for the sake of doing *something*. (Many people drift into teaching *'because I couldn't think of anything else to do'*.)

3.   The more you know what you want out of life, the more likely you are to achieve it, even if it takes years to get there.

4.   Planning ahead and knowing where you're going gives you purpose in life. You feel safer. You have a plan.

5. Your job hunting will be far more successful if you know what you want to do – it'll be easier to convince employers of your commitment and interest! Employers want whole-hearted, enthusiastic, interested people on board – not drifters.
6. Most opportunities exist for those with skills and training – zilch qualifications means fewer job opportunities. Plan your career and you'll do qualifications that are relevant to what you want.

Start your career planning by working out what you enjoy and what you're good at

We're all good at *something*. If you can build on to the bits in your life you enjoy, and are good at, you're well on the way to finding out what makes you tick. What do you look forward to in your week? What would your life be like if you could do those things all the time?

WORK IT OUT

Looking at the way forward: an action plan.

1. Focus on what you're good at, interested in and enjoy – discuss your ideas with people you know and trust.
2. Work out which skills and interests you want to use at work.
3. Build up a picture of the job market.
4. Work out where your place is in it, keeping in mind the skills and interests you want to use.
5. Look at the stepping stones you need to get there – remember they may take several years to jump over.

But always think ahead...

When I was young, I learnt to ride. 'Don't look at the ground, or you'll end up down there,' my riding teacher would roar at me. 'Look ahead to where you want to be and you'll get there.' Amazingly, I always did end up where I wanted to go when I looked in the direction I wanted to go.

The same is very true of your future. Have a vision, a picture of where you want to go, and you're far more likely to end up there.

SUMMARY THOUGHTS

☐ Loads of people change career. A career choice you make as a teenager or a graduate won't mean you're set for life in one job. *Expect* to change career three or four times in your working life.
☐ We all spend a lot of time at work, so it's important to get a job you'll enjoy and be good at.
☐ The worlds of work and education have changed: you'll need to move with more direction after school than people did a few years ago.

| Q | Summary Exercises |

Look back at the six reasons to plan your career on pages 8 and 9. Now tick A or B:

A.   Do you want real control of your life...
B.   ... or to just drift through it?

A.   Do you want to force the pace of your career...
B.   ... or just go with the flow?

A.   Do you want to spend your life doing things you enjoy and are good at...
B.   ... or do you want a job just for the sake of doing something?

A.   Are you feeling more positive about choosing a career now
     than you were when you chose your current course...
B.   ... or does it not bother you?

A.   Do you want your career to be a blast? *'Wow! I love this.'*...
B.   ... or a bore? *'Isn't it time to go home yet?'*

If you scored mostly As, you're all set to make a career choice
and get on with the exercises in this book. If you're more on
the B side, look again at the six reasons for planning your career.

CHAPTER TWO

Strategies for coping while deciding

top T I P

Don't think you have to come up with one job you want to do. Think of a sector of work, or industry, you'd like to work in and what's important to you in life and work.

Instead of saying 'I want to be a nuclear engineer' or 'I want to be a graphic designer', look at the *sectors* of work or industries, or parts of the economy or society, that interest you: 'I'd like to do something in engineering' or 'I'd like to do something connected with design.' It's much easier to think broadly about sectors which interest you, rather than trying to pinpoint one particular job from all the thousands on offer. Most jobs change, anyway, over a period of months, and employers want to recruit people who show a real interest in the sector or industry they're applying to work in.

To kick off, look at things that you have a natural interest in. What sorts of things give you a buzz, a feeling of excitement, a wish to get really involved and passionate? Why should you start here when thinking about your career? Well, we're all spending longer hours at work, for starters, so it's important to find a job in an area that interests you. You'll be more likely to want to read up on new technological developments, services, products and competitors, so you'll be better able to provide your customers with informed help and the commitment they expect. As you go higher up into management or consultancy, it will be even more important to read widely around your sector, so that you can help your company to develop and compete successfully.

top T I P

Commitment, enthusiasm and *an interest in what you're doing* are as important as the qualifications you have.

Look at the list of things below. Give a ✶ for those following that interest you and a ━ for those that don't. Feel free to add some more of your own.

✶ Yes, this interests me	━ Not likely!
the sea, the ocean	how computers work
finding out how things work	travel
cars	aircraft
trains	boats
people	plants
science	current affairs
financial world, money making	houses, buildings
design	outdoors
sport	colour
textiles	fashion, hair, beauty
improving people's lives	world peace
living conditions	art
music	the past, history
the Internet	crime, mystery

✸ Yes, this interests me	— Not likely!
how other people live(d)	books, reading
technical things	the stars (in the sky!)
how the earth works	hygiene
food	reading, books
motorbikes	animals
children	elderly people
relationships	how the body works
building things	how things are made
the land	crafts
danger	languages
law	health
drama	how the mind works

The workplace is divided into sectors or industries. Every sector offers a whole range of job opportunities. There's a list below. Looking at the interests you've put a ✸ by, match them to the sectors below as closely as you can.

Ring in red: *'That sounds good'*, or *'That's for me!'*
   the ones that are a close match.
Ring in blue: *'Hmm, maybe…'*
   the ones which sort of match.
Ring in black: *'No thanks – not in a million years.'*
   No match that you can see at all!

- ☐ Caring for people
- ☐ Business, management, consultancy
- ☐ Art, design
- ☐ Teaching
- ☐ The media
- ☐ Animals
- ☐ Entertainment
- ☐ Leisure
- ☐ Hospitality, catering
- ☐ Health, medicine
- ☐ Information technology
- ☐ Social services

☐ Law
☐ Security
☐ Money/finance
☐ Selling, retail, buying
☐ Earth/ocean science
☐ Science
☐ Engineering
☐ Transport
☐ Construction
☐ Land
☐ Nature, plants
☐ Manufacturing, making things
☐ Other

Many of these sectors – but not all – can be entered into after university if you are willing to undertake further training and/or studies.

top T I P

Build up your knowledge of sectors that interest you (the ones you ringed in red). You can't do that without research.

This is going to take time. The exercises in this book will help you work out what's important to you in a job, a company and life. As you find out more about the sectors which interest you, you can pinpoint the opportunities which are going to give you just what you want.

Get your supporters together

Your friends and family want to help you choose the right direction. And you know, you need your supporters, people who are going to make you feel good about yourself. Your mum? Dad? A carer? Your grandparents? Uncles/aunts? Friends? A particular teacher or tutor? Someone you've worked for, or done a few odd jobs for?

---

i

INFORMATION POINT

Where can I find out about sectors?

- Read the papers, especially anything relating to the sector that interests you. Do you feel strongly about what you've read? Do you want to read more?
- Look up the major players in the sector (you can get their names from the articles you read). Visit their Web sites. Do they have information on their Web pages about working for them?
- Flick through your local copy of Yellow Pages. Which local organizations are involved in the sector? Pay them a visit if you can, or call and ask for any careers literature they may have. Ask your careers service what sort of people the organizations might recruit.
- Look in your careers library for the Kogan Page series *Working In* and *Great Careers for People Interested in*. University careers libraries have the Hobsons *Casebooks* which have tons of information and case studies.
- Get work experience in the sector, even at the lower levels. Talk to people working in the sector. Do they enjoy their work? How did they get to where they are? Read through the trade magazines that careers services and public libraries have on display.

Even if they're out of touch with the job market, you can still ask them to help you pinpoint your qualities and interests. In other words, you can ask them what they think makes you the person you are. Talk to your supporters about your career plans (they don't have to be family members). They'll be flattered when you ask them for help and advice.

Some will say to you: *'It wasn't like this in my day.'*

'Yup,' you think, *'I know – I've heard it all before.'* This time, they're right. When older people were your age, the world was

very different. So were the rules by which you got a job, planned your career, lived in a relationship and lived life. Always get up-to-date information from professional bodies and careers services when planning your career.

And now, here are some tips for handling 'The Pains' – the not-so-helpful people

Although you'll have your supporters, you may also have people who aren't going to be so positive. So here are some ways to handle them without telling them where to go.

'That's that decided, then. Good.'

The minute you mention a career, some people may think you've made your mind up. They're so pleased you've 'finally decided what you want to do' that they tell all their friends. Unless it's something they disapprove of. Tell them you're keeping your options open and checking out jobs similar to the one you've already mentioned, that you need to think widely so you don't close any possibilities out.

'I wish they would stop asking me what I'm going to do!'

WORK IT OUT

Handling relatives:

- Sit down with them, or the person you trust most.
- Tell them that you appreciate the interest everybody is taking. *'It's nice to know people are thinking about me.'*
- Explain they're putting pressure on you and not helping – they may not realize the effect they're having on you.
- Tell them what you're doing to plan your career – show them this book, for starters!
- Give them a job to do. *'What would really help me is if you could…'*

That said, don't let them do all your research for you. You have to react to information honestly yourself; your relatives and friends aren't *you*. They might think it would be *lovely* if you could be a physiotherapist, dog walker, astronomer. The very thought might make you go green: you don't like people who are ill, or dogs, and the only stars you're interested in are the ones in your mag/paper telling you what sort of a month/week you're going to have. *But they don't know that.*

  'It's just a phase she's going through, really. She'll grow out of it.'

People who say this are trying to reassure themselves you're still a child and they're not that old, really. That, or they're not listening to you one jot. They're likely to be saying the same thing in 30 years' time. Don't waste your life by trying to please them.

Judy wanted to go into engineering, and preferably into management. She was studying maths, physics and French at A Level, and her dream was to study civil engineering and work in France. Her mother was horrified at the thought of her daughter becoming an engineer, largely because she knew so little about it herself. Judy pursued her goal, writing to the professional associations and also to universities for course literature. She left it lying around at home and her mother, curious, started to read it. Gradually she came round to her daughter's ambitions – especially when she had the chance to visit Judy in Paris while she was on work experience.

┌─ **WORK IT OUT** ─┐

Deal with the 'Oh, she'll grow out of it' by:

- ■ proving to yourself that the interest is for you;
- ■ checking out the careers related to it;
- ■ building a network of people who'll encourage you;
- ■ taking the whole thing seriously;
- ■ remembering that you're the one who'll be doing it, not your mum, aunt or anybody else.

'You'll come into the family business, won't you – it would be nice to keep it in the family.'

I'll probably go into my father's business – I know that's what he wants and I'd hate to let him down. It also saves me from thinking about the future.

Ari

Go into my mum's business? No way! I want to have my own!

Lucy

┌─ **WORK IT OUT** ─┐

Telling them you have other ideas:

- ■ Sit down with your mum/dad. Share your career thoughts with them so they feel included.
- ■ Tell them you might join later – after you've got experience elsewhere. They'll benefit from your fresh approach!
- ■ Don't worry that you're letting them down by not joining the family business.

My mother has her own business – but I wouldn't join that straight away. I'd want to do something else first and get experience and then go into it; maybe I'll go to college and travel before coming home to work.

Scott

The days of people automatically joining the family business have gone. Most parents would prefer you do what you want to do. You could get useful experience by helping them out.

Don't focus on pleasing others. Focus on pleasing yourself

As kids, we seek approval from mum/dad, teachers, relatives and friends. We're encouraged to be 'good girls' or 'good boys' (reward: praise, thanks, maybe a bar of chocolate). We even do things we don't want to do to be liked and loved – even by our friends. Well, now it's time to please yourself.

If you don't learn what you want now, and what you enjoy, you'll end up pleasing others for the rest of your life. Do you want a career as a doormat?

WORK IT OUT

Please yourself:

- Be honest with yourself – listen to your gut instincts.
- Don't be swayed by others or manipulated by them – they may have their own agenda, not necessarily in your best interests.
- Don't fear disapproval – practise handling it.
- Concentrate on what you're good at and enjoy.
- Say: 'Well, we're all different – wouldn't life be boring if we were all the same?'

Use the resources available. It's your RIGHT!

'So what's on offer?'

top T I P

People are there to help. That's what they're paid for, and why they chose to go into their profession, so make use of them.

There are many people who want to help find the right career for you. Many of them work in careers services in schools, colleges and universities, and also in local careers service companies throughout the country. Their emphasis will change – for example, a university careers library will have far more detail on postgraduate courses than a college of further education – but careers services offer you the chance to get up-to-date information on careers. So careers libraries are *the* place to go for details on:

- ☐ what different jobs involve and ways to get into them, the sort of person you need to be, qualifications required;
- ☐ employment trends in your area and nationally – which sectors are expanding, which are decreasing;
- ☐ working and studying abroad;
- ☐ voluntary organizations;
- ☐ lots of ideas if you want to take a year out;
- ☐ information about work experience schemes and opportunities to find out about working in management;
- ☐ details on all the training schemes available in your area;
- ☐ advice on finding a job;
- ☐ university and college courses, including prospectuses;
- ☐ the nitty-gritty on funding if you want to take a course, and benefits;
- ☐ housing, health and counselling services in your area.

The careers services in schools, colleges and universities, and also in local careers companies, have trained, qualified and impartial careers advisers who will help you make the right choice of career and give you advice when you come to apply for jobs and courses. You'll have the chance to do computer aided guidance tests to help you determine what sort of jobs might be for you. Most importantly, you'll have the chance to sit down with a careers adviser for a careers interview, so make the most of the time you have.

WORK IT OUT

Handling your careers interview:

- Write down what you want to talk about.
- It will help you focus your mind on what you want to talk about.
- It will save you spending five minutes going *'Umm... err...'* and feeling a complete idiot.
- Remember, these people are trained and qualified to help people just like you.
- Careers advisers have heard it all before – your thoughts won't sound stupid to them.

Please don't think your career will be mapped out as a result of one half-hour careers interview. You will get an action plan – a summary of the points you've discussed and a list of the things you need to do next. You may need to go back several times to see an adviser. If you don't feel comfortable with the adviser you're given, ask for another next time you call for an appointment.

top T I P

Your careers service is open throughout the holidays and half-term. People will be there to help you, so go and keep them busy.

Within your courses, you'll have teachers or tutors who know you well; and who've seen enough of your work and you to help you in deciding your strengths and weaknesses. Finally, don't forget:

- ☐ Newspapers – all full of tips about work and finding jobs.
- ☐ Careers fairs, exhibitions with universities, colleges, sixth forms and employers.
- ☐ Employers – many have brochures and Web sites outlining their career opportunities.
- ☐ The Internet – check out employment, jobs, careers, careers services. Go surfing. See what you can find.
- ☐ Professional bodies set educational, training and ethical standards for different careers. Careers libraries have their addresses.

BE REALISTIC

'Why are our expectations of what I can achieve so different? Why can't they just accept me for what I am?'

Most educational establishments and parents push you to get the best results you can. Here's why:

- ☐ Schools, colleges and universities want to make a good showing in the league tables.
- ☐ They want to help you reach your full potential.
- ☐ Parents want you to have more opportunities and choices than they did.

Many parents want to bask in your glory and tell all their friends how well you've done, but they'd never admit it, and might not even realize it. Parents shouldn't live out their dreams through you. Tell them to get a life of their own! They'll still be talking about you and what you're doing when they're in a nursing home, as they dribble and slurp their soup. Let them get on with it. Do the best you can *for you*.

You should be realistic, too, about what you're likely to achieve. I'm not saying, don't aim high. Know your strengths – *and* your limits. Privately, most of us know in our hearts when we're not going to make it. If you want to be the next Alan Shearer or Andy Cole, but can't make the school football team, that should be telling you something. If you want to be a pilot, but your grasp of science is zilch, think again. Look for another way to get involved.

Try things out. Experiment

The more you try out new things, the more you can find out where your strengths and interests are. It's like trying out a new style of clothing. You won't know if something is right for you until you try it.

Friends are important to all of us, but so are our own values, interests, needs and surroundings. Take time to try things out and work out what's important to you. Of course, you might say, *'Well, none of my friends are doing anything about their careers, so I'm not going to, either.'* Want a bet? Listen to Shauna:

> I finished my course – I'd done nothing about applying for jobs, hadn't even thought about it. It was a shock when most of my friends admitted they had jobs to go to – they'd all been visiting the careers library, sending off applications, having interviews. I didn't even know where the careers library was.

'*You need to experiment a lot to find out more about yourself, so you know what you're looking for, and what makes you tick and gives you that spark...*'

The range of activities you might get involved in is endless, but some suggestions are:

☐   doing voluntary work;
☐   organising some work experience;
☐   joining clubs and societies, especially if you can take on a position of responsibility like treasurer, secretary or fund raiser;
☐   trying out new hobbies;
☐   getting stuck into new interests;
☐   signing up for a new course;
☐   meeting new people;
☐   being open minded!

Employers will look at your CV for involvement in these sorts of things for evidence of your personal skills and strengths.

---

i

INFORMATION POINT

Find out what's on offer in your area.

Check:

■   your youth service or Student Union;
■   the local papers;
■   your church;
■   community service organizations;
■   Yellow Pages in the phone book;
■   your tourist office, if you have one;
■   Citizens' Advice Bureau;
■   notice boards at school, college or university;
■   local library or in the village hall. They'll have details about the different activities and clubs around;
■   the Internet.

Practise stress management!

You're probably going through a very stressful time, so here are:

 cheap ways to *unwind*...

1. Get some exercise and fresh air – go for a walk, even if it's just for 10 minutes. *Feel* the power of exercise.
2. Talk to someone you trust about any worries you have – especially financial ones. Don't let problems get bigger than they need to be – stamp on them while they are small.
3. Have a nice long soak in the bath. *Feel* the water soak into those pores.
4. Watch a comedy on telly. *Let yourself go*. Have a laugh.
5. Treat yourself. *Gorge* on your favourite bar of chocolate.
6. *S-t-r-e-t-c-h* from top to toe – feel the blood run through your veins.

SUMMARY THOUGHTS

You've got opportunities to try new things out – they won't be so easy to access again. Experiment – and you'll know what you like and don't like.

You're an individual. Work out what's right for you. This takes some people longer than others. But we all can get there in the end!

 Summary Exercises

Okay, here are some practical things to do. You'll need to make friends with your careers library, so get down to it:

1. Go to your careers library.

If you are at school or college:

☐ find and learn how to use *Occupations*;
☐ ask to see ECCTIS 2000, a *fast* way to get up-to-date information on computer;
☐ find out what the CLCI system is and how it works;
☐ surf the Internet for *careers* or *employment* or *jobs*. Get to know the sort of help you'll get from it.

If you are at university:

☐ visit the Prospects web site;
☐ familiarize yourself with the facilities your careers service has;
☐ find out about the calendar for recruitment.

2. Visit your local careers service and:

☐ ask what they can do for you;
☐ find out if they have a Web site and, if so, get their address;
☐ note down their opening hours;
☐ take a look at the job vacancy board;
☐ ask which jobs are expanding in your home area and nationally;
☐ get information on the training schemes available in your area.

3. List everybody you know who's working.

☐ Make a note of their names and the sort of work they do.
☐ Start talking to them when you see them about their jobs, their sectors and how they got to where they are.

4. Get to know what's available in your home town.

☐ Study the recruitment pages in your local papers.
☐ Compare them with national papers, like *The Guardian* or *The Times*.

Tuning into
You, Plc

Everything you do in your spare time will help guide you to the sort of sector to work in. You might want to go into management, but in what sector of the economy? The travel industry? Finance? Property? Engineering?

Finding your own niche is important if you want to enjoy working. So this chapter will help you work out:

1. your hobbies, interests, voluntary work and talents;
2. what you do well – your skills and strengths – to see which ones you'd like to develop and use at work.

top T I P

Spare-time activities all hold a key to your future career because you're *choosing* to do them, so they must mean something to you.

| Q | **What are your favourite hobbies?** |

1. _____
2. _____
3. _____

Have you thought about doing some sort of work related to your hobbies? (Hobbies, by the way, include the time you spend meddling, tinkering, fiddling with things, eg putting on make-up, mending a bike, looking after pets, listening to music, working on a car engine, designing cars and hanging out with friends.)

Hobbies and interests are *big* business. People turn to clubs, organizations, retail outlets and knowledge specialists for information, advice and goods, all related to their hobbies. These organizations need staff. If you love football and have a wider interest in sport generally, plus you enjoy selling things and passing your knowledge on to people, what about a career in retail sports outlets? You'll meet people with similar interests and they'll remember you for your enthusiasm and natural interest. If you enjoy writing, observing, researching and reporting, and you can find a new angle to something, why not consider a career in journalism as a sports reporter?

Here are some more examples of hobbies that could turn into careers:

If you like to spend your time	**You could look at working in these sectors**
☐ doing your friends' hair and make-up	*hair and beauty, retail, leisure*
☐ mending friends' bikes/cars	*engineering*
☐ designing computer programmes, computer games	*IT industry*
☐ visiting elderly people	*caring industry, health sector*
☐ playing the stock market	*finance sector*

If you like to spend your time	You could look at working in these sectors
☐ debating	*law*
☐ writing articles for the local press	*media, journalism*

WORK IT OUT

Look for sectors connected to your hobbies.

- ■ Check the Yellow Pages for any businesses related to your hobby too; eg don't just check 'football'; look under 'sport' and 'leisure' as well. They all need staff.
- ■ Check the Internet for details of companies nationally and internationally. Do their Web sites have information on working for them?

USING TALENT

Some areas of work demand a very high talent ability to take your interest to a professional level, like sport, music and art. If you have a flair for music, you might become a professional – a singer, composer, conductor – or use your interest in music as part of your work, perhaps working for an orchestra organizing their tours, promoting the calendar of events at an arts centre.

Marianne did a business studies degree. She loved all sorts of music, having played the clarinet and got all her exams. She got involved in many musical societies at uni. After graduating, she got a job working for an arts centre. This meant she could do work which interested her – music, arts and performing – and put her business studies degree to good use – budgeting, promoting, organizing and selling.

Only you can determine whether you want to take your talents on:

☐ to the professional level;
☐ as a hobby, enjoying them in your spare time;
☐ as part of a job where the interest is essential to do the job properly.

Talk to specialist teachers, tutors and coaches to help you determine if you're likely to get to the top and get the low-down on what you'd need to do. Be realistic. And good luck!

 Track your week for clues of what interests you and what you enjoy

What sorts of things do you feel strongly about? The environment? Child abuse? Politics? Land conservation? Farming rights? Building bridges? Do you want to make a difference to anything and leave your mark on a particular area of life which you feel passionate about? These can all lead to future careers in environmental sciences, social services, the law, politics, estate management, land conservation, agriculture, engineering ... to name just a few. Think about what you argue about most with your friends, or whether there's any area of life where you'd really like to make a difference and leave your mark.

Voluntary work can lead to careers

If you enjoy mowing people's lawns, looking after animals, fund-raising, promoting awareness of international problems, making cakes for jumble sales – all these sorts of activities can show the way to a range of careers if you enjoy them and want to get more involved.

Examples of voluntary activities becoming careers include:

☐ visiting the elderly   *care sector care assistant in a*
                          nursing home or hospital; health
                          visitor; social worker; health
                          management

☐ raising money   *charity fundraising*

☐ looking after animals   *kennel owner; groom; office*
                          manager

☐ promoting international *international organizations;*
   problems, eg welfare of *politics; third world*
   prisoners   *development; lawyer*

☐ running the school bank *banking; finance; insurance;*
                          building societies

I spent a lot of my time in the sixth form working at a women's hostel. It meant I could get a lot of experience, and I became fascinated by issues facing women. Now I'm going to do a social policy course at uni, concentrating on support for women who've suffered from domestic violence. If I hadn't got involved in the voluntary work at the start, though, I'd never have thought of it.

Anita

Voluntary work matters, especially to employers looking for people who really care and are committed about helping others. Doing the dirty work shows you've got the commitment, all right.

top T I P

Voluntary organizations need all sorts of staff, from paid professionals to volunteers. Might they hold a future for you?

Look through the recruitment pages in *The Guardian* newspaper to get an idea of the range of opportunities in the public and voluntary sectors.

 So how passionate are you about your hobbies, talents and interests?

Take each of the hobbies, talents, interests and voluntary work you do. Test how passionate you are about each one by doing this quiz:

_____ Do you read about it at every chance you get?

_____ If you won the National Lottery tomorrow, would you still be involved in it?

_____ Are you well up to date with all the latest news and changes?

_____ Do you practice it/get involved with it at every chance you get?

_____ When your coursework is done, is it the first thing you turn to?

_____ If you were to walk into a library, would the section relevant to your hobby/interest be the first one you go to?

_____ Do you spend a lot of time meddling with it, doodling about it or thinking about it during lessons or lectures?

_____ Would you rather be doing your hobby/interest than doing anything else?

_____ Would you have the talent to do it full time?

_____ Would you want to develop your hobby/interests further into a career?

If you scored:

8–10 ticks This could be the career for you!

5–7 ticks   Have you thought about work related to your hobby or interest? Like a lawyer who specializes in domestic violence cases?

2–4 ticks   Why not keep this as something you can enjoy and relax from?

1 tick   Is this really a hobby/interest? Or are you winding yourself up?

ARE YOU A TELLY ADDICT?

'Some television programmes give valuable insight into different careers or give you fresh ideas to think about.'

An example? The BBC showed a series of programmes *Working in Engineering* in October 1999 – invaluable for anybody interested in becoming an engineer or who wanted to see what the sector could offer them.

If you spend all your time watching telly, look at the sort of programmes you like to watch – they might give you clues as to what your interests are, or inspire your career thoughts. Look at the skills and qualities the TV characters need to play their part. Would you want the sorts of pressures they're under? Talk to people actually doing the job to find out how realistic a picture TV paints of their career. There are also a few careers related to *watching* television: pick up any TV magazine, newspaper and women's magazine. Many have people who write updates on soaps, compose puzzles and games relating to television programmes and write sitcoms or dramas.

Fact

If you spend your time watching the box, you're not helping yourself. You won't have anything interesting to put on your CV to grab the attention of recruiters, nor will you be putting yourself into situations to boost your self-confidence and develop the skills employers want. If there's one thing selectors look at, it's signs that you do something else other than watch telly in your spare time. Enough said. Go to page 25 in Chapter 2. Get involved in *something*. Employers – especially graduate employers – want to see proof that you've got motivation, a can-do attitude and enthusiasm.

LOOK FOR SKILLS YOU USE IN YOUR WEEK

'I don't use skills, though!'

You use skills every day – you couldn't go through life without them. Here's an example.

Skill	Example
Budgeting/numeracy	*'How can I make this money last all term?'*
Assessing what to spend your money on	*'Food? rent? books? CDs? drink?'*
Communicating your needs clearly and politely	*'I'm really in debt and need to work out how I'm going to pay it back!'*
Problem solving	*'How can I sort this out? I know!'*

Here are some more examples of skills:

You	Skills you're using
Suggest something to do on a wet Saturday afternoon	*Creative, inspiring*
Get a group of you together to do something	*Motivating others, organizing, planning, recruiting the gang*
Spend time listening to your friends' problems	*Good listener, people feel easy confiding in you with their problems*
Suggest things they might wear, or make-up they might use	*Encouraging, creating, interest in fashion*
Meeting new people	*Practising social skills, relating to other people*
Solve arguments between friends?	*Negotiating, placating, solving*
Think of something to do that doesn't take much money	*Resourceful, budgeting*

You	Skills you're using
Helping friends with homework	*Developing others, helping and caring for them, coaching, mentoring*

 Look for clues of the skills you're developing

Throughout your week, you probably take part in activities in and out of the classroom, lecture hall, and tutorials. You need skills to undertake these activities. Looking at the list below, underline the ones you use, and highlight those you enjoy using the most and those you're good at using.

- ☐ making people laugh
- ☐ listening to others
- ☐ explaining things
- ☐ handling complaints
- ☐ speaking in public
- ☐ meeting and greeting people
- ☐ doing practical things
- ☐ working without supervision
- ☐ meeting deadlines
- ☐ paying close attention to detail
- ☐ handling equipment
- ☐ taking fair decisions
- ☐ making people feel welcome
- ☐ taking lots of information in
- ☐ using mathematics to solve problems
- ☐ helping people
- ☐ answering questions
- ☐ working with your hands
- ☐ handling cash
- ☐ assembling things
- ☐ listening to other people's problems

- ☐ promoting things
- ☐ reaching a high standard of work
- ☐ performing
- ☐ thinking of ideas
- ☐ leading others
- ☐ inventing things
- ☐ mending things
- ☐ writing
- ☐ designing
- ☐ enquiring into things
- ☐ organizing things
- ☐ handling several projects at the same time
- ☐ working under pressure
- ☐ researching information
- ☐ analysing information
- ☐ finding things out from people
- ☐ solving problems
- ☐ using your initiative
- ☐ making a little go far
- ☐ spotting problems
- ☐ debating
- ☐ negotiating
- ☐ nursing
- ☐ entertaining people
- ☐ handling animals
- ☐ caring for others
- ☐ handling money
- ☐ working with others
- ☐ achieving things
- ☐ delegating
- ☐ expressing your views
- ☐ drawing
- ☐ using data to present an argument
- ☐ acting as a facilitator
- ☐ presenting a case
- ☐ selling things

- ☐ fund-raising
- ☐ coping with change
- ☐ raising awareness of something
- ☐ writing computer programs
- ☐ competing for things
- ☐ getting a group of people to do things
- ☐ taking risks
- ☐ maintaining things
- ☐ repairing something
- ☐ pulling ideas together
- ☐ organizing yourself
- ☐ presenting information/ideas/things
- ☐ giving advice to other people
- ☐ remembering things
- ☐ putting people at ease
- ☐ making calculations
- ☐ making observations
- ☐ using machinery
- ☐ socializing
- ☐ coping with routine stuff
- ☐ working from technical notes/drawings to produce something

Q Look at your work experience too

What skills from that list have you used at work, be it full-time, part-time, holiday jobs, Saturday jobs, work experience organized by the school, paper rounds, baby-sitting? Underline those, and highlight the ones you enjoy using and do well.

Overall, which skills have you highlighted?

_____

_____

_____

Which skills would you want to develop further through education, training or work experience?

_____

_____

_____

Which would you want to use in the future? There may be some you're particularly good at – what about those?

_____

_____

_____

The next stage is to combine the things that interest you, plus your skills – and subject strengths – and look for careers that use them all. Here are three people who have done just that.

Sasha, aged 16, is looking at a career where she can:

☐ make a difference by doing something she feels strongly about – animal welfare;
☐ use her skills in promoting good causes and using English, her favourite subject;
☐ use her experience with horses and animals as proof of her commitment to animal welfare, and her fund raising activities in school.

She checks out the career options and comes up with several goals to get into animal welfare organizations:

Short-term goals	Check out careers info and find out about courses;
(This term)	Get interview with careers adviser; check grades I need – am I on track?

Medium-term goals (by the end of the summer)	Get exams Apply for relevant courses; get work experience over holidays
Long-term goals (next 3 years)	Complete courses in animal welfare/ PR Get job working for PR side

David is at university, brainstorming his career thoughts.

Interests/hobbies	The world of finance and money. Read the financial pages of several newspapers and follow the business pages quite closely. Tried to play the stock market, but I'm not enough of a risk taker.
Skills	Leading a team. Captain of the hockey club at uni – arrange matches, practices and social events, try to encourage new members to come along. Find it easy to get on with people of all ages. Communicate well.
Best subjects	Business studies, marketing.
Work experience	Employed in a financial services call centre one summer. Work in Student Union bar during term time and was given responsibility for rota of bar staff in third year. Ran the school bank.
Values, needs	Don't want to work for a huge organization – would prefer to remain in home region. But would like a challenge!
Career thoughts	Something in finance, preferably where I can get involved in the local community by visiting customers and meeting people. Think I'll check out working in a building society – I like the idea of managing my own team, although I also want to consider being a financial adviser.

Way forward   Visit university careers service for information. Check to see what employers there are in my home town and elsewhere. Try to get work experience over Christmas or even a few days in term time. Talk to tutors about being referees.

Kerry is looking back on her career.

Kerry loved sport at school and at university, travelling throughout the holidays and working for a hotel one summer. Her interest in the leisure industry, with her natural skills in selling and marketing, and her strong ability in maths and economics, led her to work in the leisure sector.

Career path

Broad-based *economics* degree	Education
First job in the *marketing* department of a hotel chain	Leisure – airlines
Made redundant	
Travelled again – Australia	Travel
Sales and *marketing* in a bus company	Leisure – hotels
Moved to *sales* and *marketing* role with an airline	Leisure – tour operators

Proven interest in the leisure sector

Played on many sports teams in school
Active role in sports clubs at university, developing useful transferable skills

Career strategies

- ☐ specialized in *sales* and *marketing* in the *leisure* sector;
- ☐ broadened her *experience* with every new job;
- ☐ *networked* across the sector;
- ☐ developed a *high profile* in the organization – everybody knew who she was;
- ☐ *excelled* at her job;
- ☐ took advantage of redundancies to *travel* and look at the leisure sector first-hand as a customer.

Kerry, David and Sasha have taken their interests and hobbies and put them together with their skills and subject strengths. And *wham!* They've come up with work they want to do. Did you see they both used their strongest subject in their careers? Sasha loves English, Kerry is a maths and economics fanatic and David enjoys business studies and marketing. Let's look at yours.

SUBJECTS RELATED TO CAREERS

 Checklist the subjects you enjoy and are good at

List the subjects you have studied/are studying.
    When you have done that, rank as:

Good at it	**Enjoyment factor**
A Very good at it in my group	A Love the subject
B Quite good at it	B Enjoy it
C Could do better but find it hard	C Don't enjoy it
D Hate it, no use at all	D Hate it, can't see the point

Use it in future?

A   Yes, as part of my work – eg
    science for medicine, *maths* for
    engineering
B   Sometimes, eg use *language*
    speaking to a customer
C   Occasionally, eg telling visitor
    history of area, receptionist in hotel
D   Never, thanks!

Keep studying it?
Put Yes or No

Subject	Good at rating	Enjoyment rating	Use it in future	Keep studying it
_____	_____	_____	_____	_____
_____	_____	_____	_____	_____
_____	_____	_____	_____	_____

This will help you decide which subjects you're strong in, and which you'd like to use in future and how much you'd like to use them at work. It also points you to subjects you really enjoy – though you probably know that already!

top T I P

If you are struggling with English and mathematics, get help as soon as you can to improve them. They are important subjects.

i

INFORMATION POINT

If you are at school or college:

- Look at the sectors that interest you. What sorts of subjects do you need to be good at and enjoy to work in them? Are they your strong subjects?
- Talk to students on the courses you're thinking of doing to find out how they differ to what you're doing now.
- Look at the subjects you're going to drop. Will this course of action block off any future careers?

If you're at university:

- Do you want to use the subject you've been studying at work?
- Do you want to keep studying:
  - the same subject(s) in greater depth?
  - something new at university, at postgraduate level?
  - as part of your career while you are at work eg professional qualifications?

Visit your university careers library to find out what sort of courses are on offer and to check out ways of funding them, or visit the Prospects Web site (www.prospects.csu.ac.uk).

  What about IT?

Every role around uses IT now. You can't escape it. But you can determine how much you use IT every day and how much of a focus your job has on IT.

Well, would you want to use IT as:

	YES	NO
part of your everyday work?	_____	_____
secretarial, management		
to help/support you in your work?	_____	_____
fund-raising staff who maintain databases		
of contributors		
as the business itself?	_____	_____
IT company		
as little as possible?	_____	_____
gardener who uses Excel for accounts		
to help other businesses?	_____	_____
IT consultants		

Chapter 6 will give you some hints as to ways in which you can improve your IT abilities, especially so that you can use it at work. You can check out IT careers and find out who is recruiting by exploring company Web sites, reading newspaper supplements dedicated to the IT industry as well as trade magazines. To read up on careers in computing and IT, check out *Careers in Computing and IT* by David Yardley.

WHAT SORT OF PERSON ARE YOU?

We all have a different mix of qualities which make us the people we are. Some of these are needed for certain sorts of jobs. Good book-sellers must be *friendly* and *welcoming*, so that customers will go away and tell all their friends how helpful they are; forensic scientists must be able to *pay attention to detail*; outstanding teachers are *enthusiastic* about their subject. Having these qualities means the difference between doing a job really well or fairly badly. You know how much you dread the lesson of an unenthusiastic teacher or tutor who drones on and on...

Q   **Which qualities describe you?**

☐ logical	☐ able to work quickly
☐ trustworthy	☐ confident
☐ practical	☐ agile
☐ methodical	☐ well organized
☐ stable	☐ ethical
☐ attentive to detail	☐ intelligent
☐ inquisitive	☐ has nimble fingers
☐ unsqueamish	☐ has a steady hand
☐ able to put others first	☐ observant
☐ accurate	☐ analytical
☐ courageous	☐ resourceful
☐ persistent	☐ enthusiastic
☐ fit	☐ placid
☐ dedicated	☐ conscientious
☐ strong	☐ has a sense of fun
☐ has good eyesight	☐ creative
☐ patriotic	☐ imaginative
☐ tact	☐ sensitive
☐ sympathetic	☐ able to cope with crises
☐ loyal	☐ discreet
☐ reassuring	☐ enthusiastic
☐ helpful	☐ responsible
☐ neat	☐ has a good memory
☐ has common sense	☐ healthy
☐ careful	☐ adaptable
☐ self-disciplined	☐ flexible
☐ patient	☐ strong
☐ polite	☐ understanding
☐ courteous	☐ aggressive

What does your best friend think? Does he or she agree with you, can he or she add any others? Think of your favourite teachers or tutors. What qualities do they have which makes them your favourite?

Now, think about work. Which qualities do you have that you would like to use on the job?

_____

_____

By now, you should have a really good picture of yourself and what you're good at and enjoy. This information will help point the way to your future!

FINAL POINTS

☐ The skills you use may hold the pointer for a future career – look for common themes and interests and careers/ sectors that involve or need them.

☐ Use every chance you get to try things out to find out what you like and don't like.

☐ Apply everything you're learning right now to the business world. Think: *'What jobs would need this skill or knowledge?'*

 Summary Exercises

Now summarize the exercises you've done this chapter, so that you have a whole picture of yourself as you move on. Complete the following:

I'd like to explore sectors of work which are related to these interests, hobbies and/or talents:

_____

I'd like to explore sectors of work which need these subjects:

The skills I'd like to use at work are:

I'd like to explore work which uses these qualities I have:

How I'd like to use IT at work:

CHAPTER FOUR

What do you want in life?

WHAT DOES SUCCESS MEAN TO YOU?

Work out what success means to you and you can look for the career that will give you the chance to achieve it. Success in life means different things to people. Your mates might think that being successful means having pots of money and tons of fame. You might prefer the sort of reward and success that comes from helping somebody, like...

- ☐ helping someone to stay on the right side of the law;
- ☐ talking to a pensioner who lives on her own and comes to your shop, partly to buy goods, but mainly to talk to somebody. *You're* her social life;
- ☐ seeing your class get through their examinations;
- ☐ making life more enjoyable and comfortable for a group of elderly people.

Look at three people who you think are successful – they don't
have to be famous.

☐   Why do you think they're successful?
☐   What part of their success would you like to have?
☐   What were their tactics and strategies to become successful?
☐   What do they have in common?
☐   What has this taught you about the meaning of success for
you?

Now find stories of three people in the papers or in history
who, in your view, are successful. What made them successful?

☐   desire to make a difference
☐   drive, determination
☐   focus on a project
☐   energy
☐   network of contacts
☐   high profile
☐   hard work
☐   long hours
☐   an idea
☐   financial support
☐   wealthy parents
☐   good education
☐   experience at work
☐   chance
☐   luck
☐   persistence
☐   business awareness
☐   a desire to prove others wrong
☐   a wish to serve others
☐   they love the work they do
☐   they do nothing else but work
☐   kindness
☐   doing the right thing

☐ popular
☐ vision
☐ loyalty
☐ their contribution to society
☐ other

What have these six examples of successful people taught you about success and what success means to you?

 What matters to you in life?

For some people, a balance between work and life is very important; they like to be able to have time for their friends and hobbies. Others aren't so stressed about finding a balance; their work is their hobby and takes up all days, most days. Some jobs mean the exotic holidays every year have to go, because the salary won't allow it – but the job satisfaction is high. One person wouldn't mind that, another would.

What's important in your life?

	Most important	Important	Not that important	Not at all important
My happiness				
Happiness & well-being of others				
Good health				
A certain salary				
A particular brand of car				
Own house				
Having children				
Having exotic holidays every year				
Running my own business				

	Most important	Important	Not that important	Not at all important
Friends, lots of time to socialize				
Family and pets, time for contact				
Time for voluntary work				
Time for my hobbies				
Time to enjoy myself				
A job I enjoy				
Promotion at work				
Helping others				
Using my talents				
Taking risks				
Fame				
High profile				
Winning				
Respect from others				

What would your mum/dad's answers be? Ask them!

HOW FAR DO YOU WANT TO GO?

Every sector offers lots of opportunities. Some need lots of training, tons of qualifications, a willingness to accept masses of responsibility. Others don't. How high do you want to fly in your career?

Here are some of the staff that typically make up a firm of accountants:

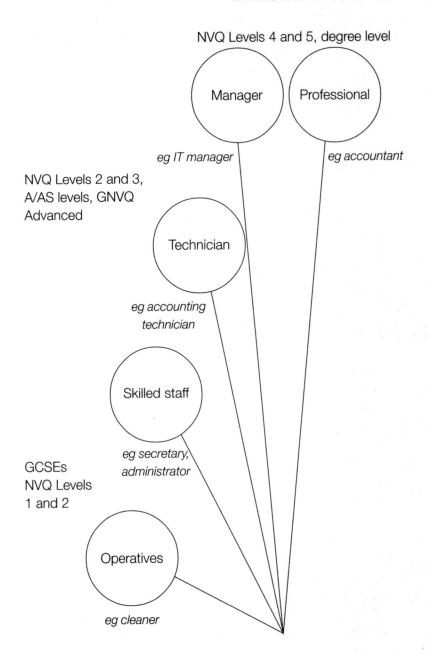

Figure 4.1 How high do you want to fly your balloon?

Go to your careers library and look up the training and qualifications required to be an:

☐ accountant, as a typical professional;
☐ accountancy technician, as a typical technician;
☐ secretary, as a skilled member of staff;
☐ cleaner, as an operative.

How do they all differ in terms of:

☐ length of training?
☐ standard of educational qualifications needed?
☐ qualifications achieved?
☐ levels of responsibility and skill?
☐ opportunity to specialize in their sector?
☐ the working day?

✓ *top* **T I P**

Many companies want to recruit staff of 'graduate calibre' or they may say in an advert 'graduate preferred'. This doesn't mean you *have* to be a graduate to apply, but it does mean that employers expect you to have the skills and qualities a graduate would have, such as an enquiring mind, and the ability to solve problems and analyze and evaluate information (amongst other things). Many investment banks want secretaries of 'graduate calibre', for example.

(You'll see that more and more people at work need to have 'soft skills' as well as specific knowledge. Engineers, for example, need strong teamworking and project management skills; lots of courses now reflect this trend. Extra-curricular activities and work experience will help you demonstrate your personal qualities, abilities and competence to an employer.)

Compare them with your own expectations of yourself and ask yourself:

A. Do you see yourself as a manager, professional, technician, skilled member of staff or an operative?

And then ask yourself that vital question:

B. Have you got what it's going to take to get there?

☐   The drive and determination to start the journey and see it through?
☐   The ability to get the qualifications you'll need?
☐   The wish for whatever level of responsibility you'll get with the job?

Look back to the people you believe to be successful. Remind yourself what it took them to make it. Have you got what it takes to make the journey down the road to success?

HOW LONG A JOURNEY DO YOU WANT TO REACH YOUR BALLOON?

Some people have a longer journey than others to get to where they want to be. A manager's training is longer than an operative's; a professional's is longer than a technician's. They will all, however, have a number of hops they need to make to get to the level they want to achieve.

The short hops are usually the bumpy bits, when you're most likely to say to yourself, *'What the hell am I doing this for?'* and wonder if you'll ever get there. It's a bit like a marathon runner, knowing he's only on mile six and there are another 20 to do. In his mind, he sees the finishing tape. The vision drives him to complete the race.

If you want to train for a profession, like architecture, medicine, surveying, accountancy, law, etc, Figure 4.2 shows what your hops might look like to get there.

People gunning for non-professional work will probably get to where they want to be much faster.

So you see, it all depends on what you want to do.

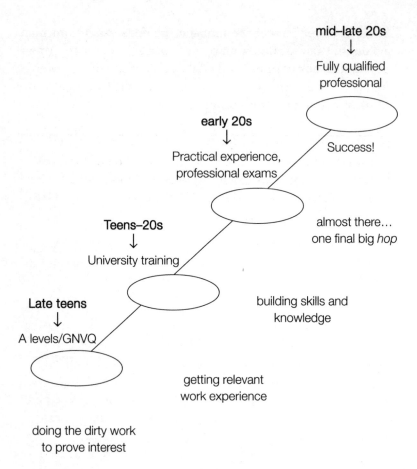

mid–late 20s
↓
Fully qualified
professional

Success!

early 20s
↓
Practical experience,
professional exams

almost there...
one final big *hop*

Teens–20s
↓
University training

building skills and
knowledge

Late teens
↓
A levels/GNVQ

getting relevant
work experience

doing the dirty work
to prove interest

Figure 4.2 How long a journey do you want to reach your
balloon?

top T I P

There may be several ways to reach a long-term goal.
Check with your careers service to find out what's
available in your area so that you can work out the best
route forward for you.

Some people find their preferred route (let's call it their plan A) doesn't work out, so they have to take a diversion (their plan B, the fall back position) which could bring other rewards in itself. A chat with your careers adviser will always help you think about other routes in.

I wanted to be a fireman. I couldn't get into our local fire service – my careers teacher suggested I look at the RAF. They accepted me – and now I've done my training – and I'm waiting to hear about my first posting!

The morale of this tale is: *Be prepared to take a diversion – think laterally and you'll increase your chances of getting to where you want to go.*

To test your motivation to keep learning, try this quiz:

| Q | **Do you enjoy learning?** |

_____ Do you like to read about your favourite subjects without prompting?

_____ Do you enjoy learning new skills?

_____ Do you like asking lots of questions and learning from others?

_____ Do you enjoy seeing new places?

_____ Do you like watching television programmes like documentaries?

_____ Do you find it easy to retain knowledge?

_____ Do you enjoy learning from the Net?

_____ Do you look forward to your favourite lessons/ lectures?

_____ And to doing coursework for your favourite subjects?

_____ Do you enjoy the hands-on practical approach to learning?

If you had:

7+ ticks: You enjoy learning – more training and qualifications shouldn't be a problem for you!

4–6 ticks: Talk to your teachers/tutors about which methods of learning are best for you and how much longer you should remain in full-time education.

0–3 ticks: It looks as though you've had enough of being in the classroom for now! Talk to your careers service about other options.

 How much responsibility do you want to have?

Some people enjoy lots of responsibility, while others are happy to sit back and let other staff members handle the heat. Let's test your willingness to take on responsibility and see how you enjoy it.

Do you:	**Yes/No**
Willingly take on positions of leadership: team captain, school prefect, club president?	_____
Like advising and helping others?	_____
Enjoy being in charge?	_____
Welcome the chance to take control of something?	_____
Like inspiring and encouraging others?	_____
Love achieving things?	_____
Enjoy getting results?	_____
Happily look for new challenges?	_____
Accept that you're wrong?	_____
Always do your best?	_____
Appreciate the importance of the things you do?	_____

How many yesses did you get?

9+ You've got 'leadership material' – you're happy to take on responsibility – just what graduate employers, the professions and the armed services need.

6–8 You enjoy some responsibility but not all the time. Perhaps working your way up to a supervisor/junior manager might give you a taster for it?

3–5 Perhaps you're more of the support player on the team.

0–2 Can you take responsibility for your own life, never mind anyone else's?

Employers and course selectors love to see out of school/ college activities on your CV – it shows you have a get-up-and-go approach. Plus, taking on positions of responsibility gives you a chance to find out how much you enjoy responsibility, and whether you'll want lots of it at work! Some people are just as happy getting on with the job in hand without all the responsibility that could come their way.

 What is important to you?

Do you want to be saying to friends in the future any of the following phrases (or something similar)?

'I sell my skills and expertise to other companies.'
'I run my own business.'
'I run a large company, accountable to the shareholders.'
'I've got my own computer company. We do project work for other clients.'
'I'm now a partner in the firm.'
'I play an active role in the community.'

'I made a difference to that person's life.'
'I love making things, working with my fingers and hands – it's really satisfying.'
'Seeing the kids' happy faces says it all.'
'I contribute to community life.'
'I really am career-oriented.'
'I've just been promoted again.'
'I adore being at work – it's my hobby.'
'I always enjoyed helping people who needed it.'
'I adored taking risks.'
'I loved being in charge.'
'I made a difference.'
'I made that.'
'I sell those.'
'I designed that.'
'I was involved in that deal.'

So you want to make a difference? To what? Look back to your original list of interests in Chapter 2 – the ones you gave a ✶ to. Any of those? This will guide you as to the sort of work you might want to do and the organization you might want to do it for.

HOW ENTREPRENEURIAL ARE YOU?

Do you want to run your own business when you're older? You might do already! There are many ways you can earn money through entrepreneurial activities, and they signal to employers that you have a get-up-and-go approach, you're prepared to get out there and take risks.

I often look for people who've done a paper round or worked part-time when I'm recruiting youngsters. It shows that they've got motivation – that they can get up and do things as opposed to spending an extra hour in bed or hanging around the shopping centre. It also shows they're not afraid of hard work.

Phil
Garage owner

You can start a business by selling a product or service, or by selling a particular skill or knowledge that you have. You may have done so already! Here are some examples:

☐ offering a personal service, such as babysitting, mowing lawns, cleaning cars and walking dogs for people;
☐ selling particular skills you have, such as writing computer programs or tutoring in your stronger subjects.

They'll help you develop skills, like being able to spot a business opportunity and to sell a service and/or product, gain confidence, and give you practice in running your own business.

INFORMATION POINT

Check out more details about being an entrepreneur.

■ The Prince's Trust helps people aged between 18 and 28 to set up and run their own businesses (see 'Useful addresses').
■ Read the book *Great Ideas for People Interested in Being an Entrepreneur* – see 'Further reading'.

If you're interested in running your own business, look for articles about people who've done it before; see how they did it. Some colleges and universities run courses about running your own business. Your bank will have useful information, too. Many people working in the personal service sector have their own businesses, such as dog walking, offering massage, aromatherapy, sandwich rounds, crafts, hairdressing services... Got any other ideas?

MONEY MAKES THE WORLD GO ROUND

'I want to get rich.'

top **T I P**

One in 500 people in this country is a millionaire. Why not you one day?

How important is money to you? What would you like that money to buy you? Which of the following sentences is true for you?

☐ I'd like a lifestyle such that I never have to work again. (Remember, most of us couldn't live without work of some sort – we need to feel needed.)

☐ I'd like a comfortable lifestyle, so that I didn't have to worry about money, but I'd still have to work.

☐ I'd like enough to get by on every month.

☐ I don't care about money – job satisfaction and doing something I love is far more important.

In many voluntary organizations, the pay isn't so great, but people get their real satisfaction from their knowledge that they're helping others – that's where the real reward is. Many groups offer good perks, which help substitute for some of the pay cheque. Increasing numbers of people retire from business life at 50+ to join the voluntary sector, offering their experience and skills to worthy causes.

> INFORMATION POINT
>
> Check out more details about working for voluntary organizations/charities.

Check out *The Guardian* newspaper on a Wednesday, which has lots of information about working for the public and community sector. Many charities also advertise in Monday's edition, where they are seeking PR and sales and marketing people who'll help them raise their profile.

> *top* **T I P**
>
> There are many examples in the press of people under 30 who are striking it rich through their own efforts. They are focused and know where they're going. You can, too, if you have drive to succeed and a passion for what you're doing.

FINAL POINTS

Think about what success means to you, and what's important to you in life. This will tell you what sort of organization you want to work for and the sort of work you want to do.

For many people, money is not as important as job satisfaction.

$\boxed{Q}$ **Summary Exercises**

What sort of success do you want to have in your life?

_____

_____

_____

_____

_____

How far do you want to go up the career ladder and how much responsibility do you want to have (ring one/two)?

Professional? Managerial? Technician? Skilled worker? Operative?

How do you want to make a difference?

_____

_____

_____

_____

_____

How much training are you prepared to do to get there?

_____ Whatever it takes.
_____ Absolutely no more than three or four years.
_____ Just a couple of years' full-time education – prefer to train on the job, if I can.
_____ I want to go out to work at once, and learn on the job.
_____ Just enough practical training to be able to do the job, such as a short course.

CHAPTER FIVE

Working out what you want from a job

Every job has pros and cons. A job may look glamorous and sexy, but somewhere it will have its downsides, too – they all do.

top T I P

An important part of any careers decision is to weigh up the pros and cons. Then you can decide how much the cons really do bug you and whether the pros outdo them.

WEIGHING UP PROS AND CONS

Even senior staff making a career move to another company will talk discreetly to people they trust about the pros and cons of such a move. So talk to people at work. What do they think about their jobs? What are the pros and cons? For starters, here are a few:

Type of work	Pros	Cons
Working outside	Nice on warm, sunny days	Cold and wet in winter
Working for yourself	Own business, you make the decisions	No one to bounce ideas off
Working abroad	Meet lots of interesting people	Can miss family, friends and familiar things
Working with animals	The animals themselves	Handling the death of an animal, blood
Working under pressure	Can be exciting, get you going	Can be stressful

There are pros and cons to any job – we're all affected by them differently. Most gardeners love the open-air life. Some of us may find the idea of mowing lawns and tending shrubs on a warm, sunny day appealing, until we remember that work has to be done on a cold, miserable, wet winter's day as well. So:

1. Talk to many people who work in the sectors which interest you.
2. Find out what they honestly think about the work they do.
3. React to what you're hearing – *'That's for me'* or *'No thanks.'*
4. Remember that what suits one person won't suit another.

WHAT SORT OF ORGANIZATION DO YOU WANT TO WORK FOR?

Size can make a difference in the case of your careers choice.

Small company
Might share kitchen and loo facilities with other companies; based in two or three rooms. One/two bosses.

Fairly relaxed recruitment procedures: you send in a CV, they decide whether to interview you or not.

Lots of variety with one person taking on several roles – fabulous learning experience.

Training likely to be on the job, plus college courses.
Fewer opportunities to lead others.

Large global organization
One department might take up the whole floor or a whole building.
Manager/supervisor for each department. The boss? Who's that?
Rigorous application procedures through personnel – psychometric tests, interviews, assessment centres, application forms.
Usually people work in one department, focusing on one role, eg lending, mortgages, customer service (banks).
May have entire in-house training department.
More opportunities to lead a team.

| Q | How big a company do you want to join? |

	YES	NO
a small company – say 1 to 20 people	___	___
a company with under 100 people	___	___
a medium-sized company – 100+	___	___
a company in the FTSE top 100 or 200	___	___
a family firm	___	___
one member of staff: you	___	___

Look through newspapers to find a listing of the FTSE 200. What sort of companies are listed? Now look at your local Yellow Pages. What sorts of companies exist there? Compare them.

'What sort of organizations are out there?'

1. Government-run offices, such as local education authorities, health trusts, local councils offering a wide range of services to the public; also national bodies.
2. International committees and organizations, like the European Commission, NATO, World Health Organization and Red Cross.
3. The private sector – small companies (1–100 employees), medium-sized businesses and large companies (corporates), operating in every sector, from the small corner shop to the huge financial services organization.
4. Self-employed people, who set up their own businesses or offer services from home on a consultancy or freelance basis, family businesses and freelancers, and franchisees.
5. Charities, which employ people and use volunteers.
6. Essential services – armed services, fire, police, ambulance, intelligence, hospitals – anything dealing with defence and life/death situations.

WHAT ABOUT THE DAY-TO-DAY ROUTINE OF WORK?

 How do you see yourself spending most of your time with people?

Every job involves some sort of contact with people. Would you like to work with people (tick where appropriate):

	YES	NO
over the counter?	___	___
retail sales staff, bank cashier, butcher		
in a team of professionals?	___	___
bankers working on a deal in the City,		
doctor in an accident and emergency unit		
face to face with people?	___	___
financial adviser, medical		
on the telephone all day?	___	___
call centres, 999 staff		
through bodily contact?	___	___
nursing, massage, medical, health and		
beauty, complementary medicine		
in charge of a group?	___	___
teaching, tour guide, trainer		
assessing work done?	___	___
quality control specialists, examiners, inspectors		
as a group for a day/weekend?	___	___
trainer, outdoor pursuits teacher		
work largely on your own?	___	___
lorry driver, sales representative		
helping other companies?	___	___
IT consultants, bankers,		
accountants, consultants, public relations		
listening to others?	___	___
counsellor		
supervising others?	___	___
managers, supervisors.		

Or do you prefer to reduce your contact with people as much as possible?

I prefer things to work with, eg boat, car, microscope	___	___
technicians, engineers, maintenance staff		

	YES	NO
I prefer information to people	____	____
IT, economists, statisticians		
I prefer animals to people	____	____
zoo keeper		
I prefer figures and numbers	____	____
actuary		
I prefer plants/land to people	____	____
plant biologist		

top T I P

Develop your skills working with all sorts of people. All jobs involve working with people, even if they are 'just' your colleagues and boss. You have to fit into the team.

Q **How sociable are you?**

Do you:

____ enjoy being surrounded by people?
____ like meeting new people all day?
____ find it easy to make friends?
____ find it easy to meet new people and get on with them?
____ dislike very few people?

If you've ticked all these, you'll probably want a job where you're always meeting new people and helping them out. If you've hardly ticked any, work on improving your ability to relate to people, and look at jobs where people don't feature so much.

Q

How much action do you like?

_____ I like to be in the middle of things.

_____ I like to be surrounded by fast-paced action, where things are happening.

_____ I like to be busy and get involved in everything.

_____ I prefer to work in a quiet environment where I can get on with my work.

_____ I like to be busy and to be left alone to do what I need to do.

Q

How physical and practical do you want your work to be?

☐ Hands-on *carpenter, IT engineer;*

☐ Sports-/fitness-related *personal trainer;*

☐ Growing things *horticulturalist;*

☐ Dirty *labourer;*

☐ Driving *driving instructor, sales executive;*

☐ Walking *city guide;*

☐ Practical *chef;*

☐ Brain power *manager;*

☐ Massaging *aromatherapist;*

☐ Animal-based *zoo keeper;*

☐ Water-based *diver, marine biologist;*

☐ Demands stamina *cabin steward, army services;*

☐ Dangerous *fireman;*

☐ Sitting down for most of the day *data processor;*

☐ In one position for long time *potter, dentist;*

☐ Driving to meetings/appointments *social worker, surveyor.*

Some careers may be barred to you on the grounds of health. For example, if you have skin allergies or skin conditions, working in hairdressing and beauty that involves handling chemicals may be barred to you. A chat with your careers adviser will help you find out if any of these apply to you.

What sort of pressure do you want?

You see, there are different sorts of pressure. Let's take two people who answer the phone all day at work.

David answers 999 calls

He's often dealing with panicky, stressed, frantic people; he has to calm them down, get information from them about the situation, assess it and deal with it.

Jayne works for a call centre in a bank

She helps customers calling in with enquiries. She's under pressure to sell the bank's services and products to people who call; and she knows her calls are recorded to assess her performance.

Here are some more examples of pressures people can be under at work. Pressure isn't necessarily a bad thing; it motivates a lot of people. Think about your reaction to these types of pressure – could you handle it?

split-second decision, life and death	*air traffic control, doctors in an accident & emergency department, armed services air traffic control, veterinary science*
clinching the deal	*business staff, client relationship manager, business development manager, recruitment consultant*
helping a patient decide the right course of treatment	*medical staff*

work to be done	*amount to get through in a day*
fighting a case	*lawyer, housing officer*
deadlines	*eg journalist, articles prior to publication, new advertising campaign ready for client's inspection, seeing a building put up in a set time and budget*
hitting targets	*sales, exam results, profits*
creating something others like	*author, singer, painter, designer, architect, new hair-do – will the customer like what you've achieved in half an hour?*
handling complaints	*to be able to handle complaints from customers yourself – or do you prefer to hand them over to someone with more responsibility?*
producing new drugs	*pharmaceutical industry researchers*
making quality products	*being part of an assembly unit which has to make so many items within a certain time scale to a particular standard.*

Some people are under so much pressure they burn out *fast* – but they make a lot of money. Investment analysts can make a ton of money in the City, but many look for another career by the time they're 30.

What about risk? Do you want a job with a lot of risk in it? Some people are natural risk takers – do you think you are?

1. What was the last risk you took?
2. What happened?
3. How did you cope with the outcome? Was it as bad as you feared?

Some companies – such as large investment banks – may look for evidence of your entrepreneurial activities and times you've taken risks.

Where do you see yourself working?

Some jobs are restricted to the town, country or even the City. IT does mean that people can do business from virtually anywhere – like the fund manager who works from the shed in his garden – but that's not always practical. Are you willing to move to where the jobs are? Does it matter to you what your travel time to work is like, if you love the job? Would you move to another end of the country if the job was just what you wanted? Some people work in very remote places, like fish farmers and astronomers. Does that sound like you?

If you want to stay put at home, you may need to be more flexible about the sort of job you go for. Your careers service will tell you what sectors are expanding in your home town – get training in one of those areas and experience. You can transfer your skills to another job later. Many companies are setting up call centres in areas of the country with low unemployment; these will give you skills in handling customers, customer service, information technology and working under pressure – useful in any line of work.

| Q | **Do you want a job with an international slant?** |

	YES	NO
you work in another country, with the occasional trip home	___	___
oil worker in Saudi Arabia		
your job means you travel all the time	___	___
cruise ships, airlines, railways, buses, holidays, courier work, buyers		
where you need to know a lot about different customs	___	___
tour company, travel agency, airline staff, diplomat		

	YES	NO
work with people from different countries and cultures	___	___
hotel manager, teaching English		
you have to travel abroad frequently as part of your job in the UK	___	___
auditor, quality control		
can use your languages on the job	___	___
secretarial, translator, engineer		
you can work for a firm which will give you the chance to work abroad	___	___
accountant, corporate finance		
you have the chance to work abroad for a couple of years	___	___
au pair, civil engineer		
you can work for an international organization which is political	___	___
UN, NATO, the EU		
help under-developed or developing countries	___	___
medical corp, charity worker		
work to improve international relations	___	___
politician, Foreign Office		
you're the only European around	___	___
aid agencies		

Test yourself now to find out how international you are:

Q **How international are you?**

	Tick for YES
Do you:	
seek friends from another country?	___
Name them!	
take a real interest in worldwide events?	___
Describe an event taking place right now	

Tick for YES

find that some parts of the world interest you
more than others? _____

Which parts? What do you know about them?
enjoy listening to people who've been travelling? _____

Who've you listened to recently? Recap one of their stories...

love talking to travellers to hear about their
home countries? _____

Recall what you asked them
enjoy learning languages? _____

What are you studying at the moment? Is it for an exam, or for the pure enjoyment of it?
like to travel abroad? _____

How? As a tourist eating sausages and chips, or trying out 'their' food?
take part in exchanges? _____

How did you cope with living abroad?
have a pen friend in another country? _____

How often do you write?
offer to help newcomers to your school to
settle down? _____

Who? When? What did you do to help them?

How many ticks did you get?

8–10: You're international all right.
4–7: You'll need to expand your international activities if you
want a career that'll take you places.
0–3: There *is* life outside the UK, you know!

Fact

Larger companies have centres throughout the world.
Languages and an international outlook will be important, if
you are to work for them.

What about hours?

Do you want a job where you're willing to:

- [ ] be on call out at weekends and on holidays? *doctors, vets*
- [ ] work when everybody else has gone home? *cleaning, IT systems overhaul and maintenance*
- [ ] work shifts? *nursing, social care, IT staff, secretarial staff, call centres and customer service staff*
- [ ] arrive in first, get out last, in at weekends, call in during the holidays to check all is well? *most professional and managerial sectors*
- [ ] work very long hours, at the demands of the company/clients? *self-employed, many professionals*
- [ ] work 'normal' hours, eg 9.00 am start, 5.30 pm finish? *administrative*
- [ ] work nights? *healthcare assistants, engineers, shelf stackers.*

Fact

Customers want 24-hour service – so organizations need staffing, 24 hours a day. This means there are more flexible employment opportunities – you can work at night, weekends, daytime ... and so on. It also means you have to be more flexible in terms of the time you leave work.

 What about oddities?

Could you work:

- [ ] in a noisy environment, like a factory, or open-plan office?
- [ ] with the sound of machinery or engines?
- [ ] with needles, blood and vomit? Or do they bother you?
- [ ] at a great height, like washing windows at the top of a skyscraper? Or an architect visiting a building site?

FINAL POINTS

☐ Think about the pros and cons of each job as they come and how you react to them – especially with regards to the sort of lifestyle you want.

☐ Take any chance you get to develop skills and experience of the sort of conditions you want at work, so that you'll be less of a risk for employers to recruit – you'll know what you're letting yourself in for.

Q	**Summary Exercises**

Of all the exercises you've done in this chapter, rank the things which are most important to you about your future day-to-day work:

☐ size of company;
☐ people contact;
☐ level of action;
☐ oddities;
☐ the sort of pressure I have;
☐ location of job;
☐ having an international slant;
☐ the way I make a difference;
☐ how I see my results;
☐ the hours I work.

All these things can affect the sort of career you have and your lifestyle, so you need to bear in mind what's important to you, as we move on.

CHAPTER SIX

'So which sector and jobs are for me?'

 Q Which sectors/jobs sound good to you?

Let's go back to the list of sectors in Chapter 2. You've already highlighted some that interested you more than others. Now that you've targeted your interests, and the skills and subject strengths you'd like to use at work, and you've got an idea of where you're going, think about each sector once more.

Ring in red: *'That sounds good'* or *'That's for me!'*
Ring in blue: *'Hmm, maybe...'*
Ring in black: *'No thanks – not in a million years.'*

☐ Self-employment (A)
☐ Armed services (B)
☐ Administration, business, clerical and management (C)

- [ ] Art and design (E)
- [ ] Teaching and cultural activities (F)
- [ ] Entertainment and leisure (G)
- [ ] Catering and other services (I)
- [ ] Health and medical services (J)
- [ ] Social and related services (K)
- [ ] Law and related work (L)
- [ ] Security and protective services (M)
- [ ] Finance and related work (N)
- [ ] Buying, selling and related services (O)
- [ ] Sciences, mathematics and related work (Q)
- [ ] Engineering (R)
- [ ] Manufacturing industries (S)
- [ ] Construction and land services (U)
- [ ] Animals (W)
- [ ] Plants and nature (W)
- [ ] Transport (Y)

The letters in brackets after each sector refer to its classification in your careers library. If you want information on being an engineer, you should look under R.

DO YOUR RESEARCH

This is where the important research starts about the workplace to find your niche in the sectors you'd like to work in. There's no short cut here. Put time into building up a picture of the area of work you're interested in to make sure it's right for you. This is what you need to do next:

Stage 1

Read widely around the sectors that interest you. What jobs are available in them? Do they interest you?

Stage 2

Pinpoint the jobs in the sector(s) which seem to match your interests, skills, subject strengths and goals.

Stage 3

Get first-hand experience of the sector(s) yourself to check they're for you.

If they are	If they aren't
Stage 4 Keep using relevant skills and get experience	**Stage 4** Look elsewhere in other sectors which also interest you but get some experience in the sector – you might be surprised!
Stage 5 Plot the stepping stones you'll need to take to get there, for example, staying on in education, or joining a training scheme, or getting a job with training.	**Stage 5** Make sure you do your homework to build up a picture Go back to the ones you ringed in blue on pages 13–14 in Chapter 2. Start looking at those.

The rest of this chapter will take you through Stages 1, 2 and 3.

top T I P

Don't restrict yourself to checking out one job: look at job families. If you're checking out construction, look at: carpenter, decorator, plumber, bricklayer and so on. Think broadly. If you want to be a manager or a consultant, consider what sort of managing and consulting you want to do and the sector you want to work in.

Remember that you don't have to choose one specific job, because you can always take a broad-based course related to the sector which interests you most while you're deciding where to go next. If you're graduating and you want to go into management but you're not sure what part of it is right for you, why not think about applying for a general management training scheme? This will give you experience in different departments of a company so that you can decide which one is right for you.

Q Looking at the different roles within sectors

In the three sectors you're most interested in, brainstorm the jobs available in the sector. Do this with a friend. Here's an example – dentistry.

- ☐ dentist;
- ☐ dental nurse;
- ☐ dental receptionist;
- ☐ dental technician;
- ☐ dental surgeon;
- ☐ research;
- ☐ dental hygienist;
- ☐ lecturer in university/college;
- ☐ suppliers of dental equipment.

These jobs all need different skills, qualities, training, level of knowledge and expertise, qualifications and levels of responsibility. Every job will have:

☐   pros and cons;
☐   different levels of work and responsibility;
☐   specialist areas;
☐   opportunities in different sorts of organizations;
☐   possibly, little groups of job families.

top T I P

You need information on which to base your careers thoughts. Information gives you the power to decide what to do. If you don't get motivated and get into the careers library, you'll be stuck for information.

'What should I be looking for when I'm reading about the sector I'm most interested in?'
   Try to get a feel for:

☐   what people do at work every day;
☐   the sorts of demands and pressures they face;
☐   the qualities they need to use;
☐   the sorts of people they work with;
☐   the organizations they work for;
☐   the skills they most need;
☐   the amount of training they have to do to qualify;
☐   the sort of training they have to do;
☐   entry requirements needed.

INFORMATION POINT

Where can I find details about different jobs?

Your careers library will have tons of information; the book *Occupations* gives lots of detail. Contact professional bodies to see what careers literature they can send you; *Occupations* will have addresses.

Q **Compare this information with the stuff you've found out about *you*.**

Which careers/jobs:

☐ match the skills and qualities you most want to use at work?
☐ meet your long-term goals?
☐ will enable you to use the subjects you want to continue with?
☐ will give you the sort of lifestyle you want?
☐ will offer you the opportunities you'd like?

You'll be starting to have thoughts like...

☐ Yes, this area of work is right for me, I'm going to find out more about careers in this particular group, so that I can find out about the right courses and/or employers to apply to.
☐ Yes, this sector is right for me, not sure about specializing yet though. Wonder if there's a fairly broad way which will

keep my options open? *This might be the case if you want to enter engineering but you're not sure which sort of engineering you want to do. A degree in general engineering at uni might be the ticket.*

☐ Yes, this job is right for me. I want to work as a mechanic. What do I need to become one, again? *Okay, so you've chosen a specific job. What do you need to do to get there?*

☐ Jot down the sectors, areas of jobs or specific jobs you're looking at more closely now. Read everything you can about them. Do they still spark your interest?

START CHECKING YOUR THOUGHTS FIRST-HAND

top T I P

Talking to people and reading literature isn't enough to base a careers decision on. Get out there and see for yourself what the workplace is all about.

And...

Challenge Yourself!

Put yourself in situations to find out what the workplace is like.

Trying things out means you can turn round and say:

- ☐ *'Yes, that's definitely for me – I've always loved xyz';*
- ☐ *'I'm glad I tried that – I never thought I'd like it';*
- ☐ *'Never, ever again.'*

Information gained first-hand can stop you making the wrong decision. Think laterally, though, and a new door could open for you.

> I thought I always wanted to teach after my degree. Work experience told me it was *not* for me. I'd still like to be involved in education – maybe in the Civil Service in administration, or management, or even teaching English to older students.

So get some work experience and…

Challenge Yourself!

How much can you learn on work experience? Don't just float through the day at work. You get out as much as you put in. Make your time at work a *learning* experience.

Make your learning active. Ask questions. Talk to people about their work and the sector. What did they do to get to where they are today? How far did they plan their career? How did they get the job they are in? What advice would they have for you?

Learn from your experiences at work

Think of experience you've had of the workplace recently. (If you haven't had any, think about something you've done for other people.) Ask yourself:

☐   What have I enjoyed doing the most and why?
☐   What have I enjoyed doing the least and why?
☐   What has this experience taught me about this sector of work?
☐   What have I learnt about teamwork?
☐   Was that career/line of work for me?

Use work experience to develop your awareness of the business world – this is particularly important for graduates.

WORK IT OUT

Any time you are in the workplace, try to:

■   learn a new computer program;
■   understand the goals of the organization;
■   understand how the employees all fit into the puzzle;
■   suss out a role for yourself in it;
■   see where future business opportunities might lie;
■   see who their customers are and how the company keeps them – or loses them;
■   look carefully at the way people behave at work, such as the language they use, the way they dress, the way they treat each other and work together.

Be an ambassador for work experience:

■   turn up – don't annoy employers by failing to show;
■   be enthusiastic;
■   remember that your actions and words affect every person in the team.

Try to get some experience in the career sectors you're researching. Here's how:

WORK IT OUT

Get experience.

■ Use your holidays to get work experience – your careers service or careers teacher will help you approach employers.
■ Get a part-time job to build up the skills you need.
■ Don't forget voluntary work as a way to build up skills and contacts.

In some careers, like media, it's generally expected you'll have work experience before applying for a job. It proves your interest and gives you a chance to check that it really is for you.

'Well, you haven't got quite the right skills we're looking for.'

Too many employers whinge about first time job seekers' lack of practical hands-on experience. Too many don't offer you the chance to get it. Show some muscle and initiative – organize some work experience yourself. Go out and *get* those skills!

VOLUNTARY WORK CAN BOOST YOUR SKILLS BASE

Choose the right sort of voluntary work, and you'll be well on your way to boosting up the skills you want to use at work. As a volunteer, you might be able to develop your skills by:

☐   promoting the organization in the press and media, locally
      and nationally;
☐   marketing;
☐   training staff;
☐   managing volunteers;
☐   fund-raising money;
☐   doing administration;
☐   giving secretarial support;
☐   giving financial support.

Voluntary organizations look for evidence of commitment to
their causes, or involvement in previous charity work. Many
employers want evidence that you're committed to caring for
others; doing the dirty work is the practical bit that convinces
a prospective employer of your commitment to the sector. Plus
anything you do with a wide range of people means you're
improving your ability to relate to customers, colleagues and
patients.

'What d'you want?' People are under pressure at work. If
they're rude or abrupt, they may just be having a bad day,
wrestling with a problem or coping with a heavy workload.

WORK IT OUT

Handling people under pressure:

1.   Show that you understand people are under pressure.
      'I'm sure you're very busy...' or *'Is there a more convenient
      time for you when we can talk?'*
2.   Tell what you want *briefly*.
3.   Show that you're not a time-waster: talk about an
      article you've read relating to the work, any
      experience you have...
4.   Thank them and show them you appreciate their help.

FINAL POINTS

☐ Now that you've worked out what sector you'd like to work in, the next stage is to start looking at ways you can strengthen your chances of getting to where you want to go.

☐ Look for ways you can build on your skills, interests and talents. Chapter 7 will show you how.

Q Summary Exercises

Summarize your career thinking so far!

The sector/s I'd like to work in is/are:

_____

Jobs that will take me to where I want to be are:

_____

The jobs that match my lifestyle needs and values are:

_____

CHAPTER SEVEN

Working out where you need to go from here

At this stage, you may be thinking: *'I'd like to do something in these sectors. Still not sure what, though. I'd better do something that will steer me in that direction – but keep my options open.'*

or *'This is the sort of job I'm heading for. So I'll need to pick up the right sorts of qualifications that will help me get there.'*

or *'This is the job I want to do. All I have to do now is decide whether it's best to stay on and do more qualifications – or whether I should go straight out to work or have time out.'*

top T I P

Remember, think long-term. Look ahead at the whole picture.

What do you need to do to get to where you want to go or you think you'd like to be?

To move forward to get a job in any sector, you'll need to:

- [ ] get relevant qualifications;
- [ ] develop the right skills and the key skills;
- [ ] get training;
- [ ] acquire work experience;
- [ ] show motivation;
- [ ] put some effort in;
- [ ] plan your career;
- [ ] organize your time;
- [ ] research the sector;
- [ ] build up a network of contacts;
- [ ] use resources;
- [ ] show you care about your future;
- [ ] know your own values, strengths and qualities;
- [ ] be able to spot job opportunities;
- [ ] get an understanding of the sector;
- [ ] know how to sell yourself to an employer;
- [ ] be enthusiastic;
- [ ] know what you want in a job and company.

Although by now you've probably narrowed your career choice down somewhat, you might still want to keep your options open. Don't forget, it's fine to look at the *sector* or *industry* you want to join, as opposed to targeting one job in it. Just keep on board the sorts of skills, knowledge and qualities that sector will need so that you can work on them. You might, of course, know now exactly what sort of job you want in which case you might want to check out how you get into that line of work.

What do you need to achieve to get to where you want to go?

Talk this through with your careers adviser. Whatever stage of your education you're at, there may be a choice of options open to you, depending on your long-term career plans and the sort of career you want.

The following describes some of your options.

Stay on in education

Are there any specific courses you have to take to achieve your career goals and the sort of work you want to do? Or things that aren't compulsory, but will increase your chances of getting a job? Such as psychology, if you want to consider careers helping people? Or a language, if you want to be an engineer and work abroad? Talk to a careers adviser about this. If you're working your way through university, and want to go into business, you might want to pick up a course in business studies and/or marketing, as many employers find these sorts of skills invaluable. Don't forget that local colleges run night courses that might be very useful if you want to pick up extra skills to boost your CV.

Join a training programme

There are an abundance of these, either run by training companies, often on behalf of local authorities, or run by companies themselves. Training programmes enable you to acquire relevant experience, training and qualifications. They exist for people leaving school at 16 (the national traineeship, for example), at 18 (the modern apprenticeship) and for graduates (graduate training programmes). Some offer you challenges more quickly than others – fast track management programmes may give graduates management responsibilities within the first few months of starting work. Many graduates hope that they'll be accepted onto such a scheme, although lots of school and college leavers now choose training schemes such as the modern apprenticeship as a way of getting the experience, skills and qualifications they want, as opposed to going to university and acquiring a degree. There's a list of questions you should be asking to help you decide what to do further along in the chapter.

Get a job

Most people want a job, to get the cash coming in and start paying off their debts. The best thing to go for is a job with training, hopefully sponsored by the employer, but this doesn't always happen. You may find yourself attending training courses in your own time, after a day's work, and even paying for some of it yourself. It will be worth it in the end.

Take time out

By the time you've finished school, college and maybe university, you've been in education for a very long time. You may feel you want to do something wild and wacky for a few months, or even longer. Many employers accept that this is a good thing to do – you return to the workplace refreshed and motivated – but they still expect to see you've done something with your time during your breathing space. Taking time out needs careful planning and monitoring so that you can sell your newly acquired maturity, skills and enthusiasm to an employer more convincingly.

Running your own business – got any ideas?

It's usually best to get some experience of the workplace before starting to run your own business. That way, you can learn from other firms and people, and pick up a good knowledge of what's involved. If you've got an idea, you'll need to do market research, talk to your bank about the financial side, work out where you'll run your business from, and then go out there and sell, sell, sell. Your careers service will have more details about running your own business and local colleges often run short courses, to give you an idea of what's involved.

Go on the dole

This is not a good option, mostly because it is so demoralising for you. You get out of the routine and discipline of work; anger, frustration and feelings of worthlessness may quickly take over your life. Even when you're on the dole, while you're not searching for a job you can boost your skills – many colleges offer courses at reduced rates to people who are unemployed. Recent graduates who are looking for work can still visit university careers services and may find that they do need to do some further training to get the skills employers want.

STAYING ON IN EDUCATION

There are a wide range of qualifications available to the school and college leaver – GNVQs, A levels, AS levels, degrees, HNDs, NVQs, BTECs, City & Guilds and Key Skills are a few examples. Here are some more ideas:

☐ vocational courses relating to specific jobs, such as medicine, architecture, beauty therapy (HNDs, BTEC, City & Guilds, NVQs);

☐ broad based related courses (like GNVQs, degrees), which relate to a sector of work, such as business studies, media studies or art and design;

☐ academic subjects (A and AS levels), some of which may be new to you, such as philosophy, history or geography.

As from September 2000, there's a new curriculum designed to give you a broad education at 16+, with lots of emphasis on key skills such as communication, numeracy and IT. This will boost your chances of getting a job, but you will need to sit down with a careers adviser and discuss your future plans to ensure that you are taking the right range of courses to help you achieve your career ambitions. This is particularly the case if you have a very specific career in mind – you don't want to take the wrong courses at 16 or 18, or leave out anything that might open the doors to other things later on.

Some colleges offer taster courses for students before the course starts. They will help you make sure that the course is right for you. Choose wisely when you go into further and higher education – mistakes can be expensive.

Find out:

- ☐ Where will a degree get me? How will it help me get into the sector or line of work I want to be in?
- ☐ How do opportunities in the sector I want to work in compare at 18 and after graduation?
- ☐ What will a higher education course cost me?
- ☐ What skills do graduate recruiters want, and how can I develop them and get work experience to increase my chances of getting the sort of job I want?
- ☐ What are the alternatives? How do these compare in getting me closer to my long term goal?

You'll also need to take other factors into account when thinking about your future education.

$\boxed{Q}$ What sort of learning environment do you want to be in?

Do you want to be in an environment that is (ring the ones you want):

☐ mixed?	☐ for sixth form students only?
☐ single sex?	☐ for all ages 16+?
☐ international in outlook?	☐ specialist, eg music college?
☐ close to home?	☐ offering you the opportunity to study abroad?

☐   in your region?   ☐   large?
☐   small?   ☐   on one campus?
☐   on several campuses?   ☐   in the middle of a town?
☐   outside of town?   ☐   allowing you to follow a
                                     special interest?
☐   offering good facilities?   ☐   totally new to you?

Q   **How do you like to be assessed?**

Tick those that apply to you:

_____ I prefer to have one exam at the end of the course.
_____ I prefer to be assessed through a mixture of course work and exams.
_____ I prefer to be assessed mainly through course work, with some exams.
_____ I like to learn through computer software.
_____ I like to study at home on my own, rather than in a class of people.

If you're already at university and thinking of staying on to do more study or perhaps some research, a major consideration will be cost. Options open to you are:

☐   to continue on in full-time education to do a taught master's degree, or research degree;
☐   to start work and do a part-time postgraduate degree or distance learning course instead, which might be more flexible and would mean you can start earning and paying off your debts; many business and management degrees, for example, have been made far more relevant to the workplace and your employer might be willing to part-sponsor you;
☐   to work for a few years and then apply to do a postgraduate degree full time, perhaps with sponsorship from your employer.

Visit your university careers service early on to start researching the options and cost implications, and discuss your plans with an adviser.

But whether you're just completing your degree, or leaving school after doing GCSEs, here's:

6 | reasons *not* to sign up for a course:

- ☐ 'Because I didn't know what else to do.'
- ☐ 'The school wanted me to/my tutors wanted me to stay in the department.'
- ☐ 'My parents thought it would be a good idea – I didn't want to let them down.'
- ☐ 'I didn't know what else was available to me – it put the decision off for a bit.'
- ☐ 'My friends were all staying on.'
- ☐ 'It kept everyone at home quiet for a few months, at least until I told them it wasn't for me.'

6 | reasons to sign up for a course – any of these might apply to you:

- ☐ 'I wanted to study the subject in greater depth.'
- ☐ 'I want to be an ... and I need to go through this particular career path.'
- ☐ 'I can see where it will lead when it's over.'
- ☐ 'It will be appropriate for me – it has everything I was looking for in further/higher education.'
- ☐ 'I wanted to get more qualifications and experience of life before I started work.'
- ☐ 'I've checked all the other options, and I know it's the best one for me.'

THINKING ABOUT STUDYING A COURSE? HERE'S 10 QUESTIONS TO ASK ABOUT IT

1. What do I want to get out of any further full-time education? What are the advantages of staying on? How will further studies benefit me, my employment opportunities and my career, as opposed to going to work now?
2. What sort of options can I put together to prepare for my future career? Is there anything I have to do?
3. What options are there? How do these match my (career) interests and plans?
4. What input have local or national employers made into the course to make sure it's relevant to work?
5. What can I do after the course?
6. What work experience have the *tutors* had in this area?
7. What sorts of jobs have past students gone on to do? Which employers have taken them on? How many students have dropped out of the course? Why?
8. What sort of support will I receive?
9. What avenues am I closing off to me as a result of doing this course? Do they matter?
10. Are there any costs in doing this course? If there are, what are they and what sources of funding are available to me?

You can get the answers to these questions from:

☐ the college/university prospectus and information produced by each department;
☐ visiting the institution itself and talking to students on the course and the tutors who lecture or teach on it – most institutions have open days when you can have a good look round and ask questions;
☐ attending careers exhibitions, where you'll have a chance to compare institutions;
☐ checking out the Internet – most universities and many colleges have Web sites;

☐ looking at statistics, such as where students ended up after their courses, and the quality assessments for teaching and research.

top T I P

Lots of students have dropped out of courses because they didn't know enough about the content of the course and what it would be like before they started. Talk to the students on the courses you're proposing to study. What would their answers be to the above questions?

A WORD ABOUT HIGHER EDUCATION

Higher education is an option for everybody – at the right time for them. Where does it fit into your visions of your future? Whether you're just setting out to choose your degree course, or ploughing through your university studies right now, make an effort to find out what employers want and how you can demonstrate that you've got the skills and qualities they need.

top T I P

Don't make your long-term goal *just* 'to get a degree' or a qualification. A qualification on its own isn't enough. Compliment it by developing skills and getting work experience as well, and you'll be in a far stronger position to get that job.

Many graduate employers aren't really concerned with the subject you study, unless they specifically want to recruit people with a particular knowledge base. A flexible approach is essential, especially since there is so much change in the workplace, and employers want graduates who have got the ability to learn and acquire new skills and knowledge. They want achievers and people who will go out and make things happen, and people with skills and qualities such as:

☐   communication;
☐   motivation;
☐   leadership;
☐   enthusiasm;
☐   team working;
☐   business awareness.

In today's pressured workplace, employers are keen to recruit people who are going to be a good 'fit' with the company and the people who work there, to promote a team spirit.

Many graduates find it difficult because of their:

☐   lack of work experience;
☐   inability to link the skills they have to what their employers want;
☐   lack of knowledge about the sector they're applying to work in;
☐   failure to start career planning early on in the course.

So don't make the same mistakes!

INFORMATION POINT

Find out what graduates do:

1. Visit the Prospects Web site to have a good look at what's on offer for graduates, and the sorts of employers who are recruiting.
2. Visit your local library and look for the GET publication that lists all the graduate employment and training opportunities, or you can check it out at www.get.hobsons.co.uk. Here you'll find tons of information on courses and careers.

***top* T I P**

Choosing what to do next may seem very final because you're starting to cut down your options: it's hard to shift track once you've begun a course. Don't forget that people in their 30s, 40s and 50s do change career.

GETTING OUT OF EDUCATION AND INTO THE WORKFORCE

The good news is that many employers recruit people aged 18 after they have acquired more skills, maturity and experience of the workplace.

On the plus side, at work	But
You're definitely an adult	You won't be as free as you think from rules and regulations
You'll earn cash	You'll be expected to turn up on time
You'll get experience from day one	You may have to start off with the lower level jobs (probably), although this is not the case with some graduate training schemes
Your efforts will be appreciated	You'll have three, four or five weeks' holiday a year

Going out to the workplace is a big step. Are you ready for it?

Challenge Yourself!

Compare your current day with a working one.

Ask people at work what their day is like. Ask them about:

- [ ] the time they spend there – ask them about breaks and lunch hours;
- [ ] what is expected of them – rules and regulations, behaviour and attitude;
- [ ] the pros and cons of being at work as they see them;
- [ ] how their levels of responsibility differed to when they were in full-time education;
- [ ] how they first managed their lives when they first started work;
- [ ] how they coped and what advice they would have for you.

If you've just left school and you feel you're not ready to go to work yet, why not ask your careers service about one-year courses, or training schemes? A placement with the New Deal scheme will develop your skills in the voluntary sector, full-time training or employer workplaces. You'll get plenty of support and advice! Training programmes can help you:

☐ prepare application letters and CVs;
☐ complete application forms;
☐ prepare for interviews;
☐ think about where you want to go at work;
☐ achieve qualifications which will be relevant to your career plans.

---

i

INFORMATION POINT

There are a number of places you can look for that perfect job:

■ at your local careers service and job centre – don't forget that many have Web sites;
■ on the Internet;
■ through a recruitment agency;
■ ask everyone you know who is recruiting;
■ write directly to an employer to ask if they have any vacancies;
■ check the local papers' recruitment pages;
■ look in shop windows;
■ ask directly at local stores, banks and offices.

If you are at university, remember that:

- [ ] your careers service will have vacancy lists;
- [ ] professional bodies produce vacancy lists;
- [ ] local, regional and national newspapers have recruitment pages;
- [ ] small- and medium-sized companies make up a major part of the economy; don't forget them when you are looking for work;
- [ ] careers fairs and employer presentations are held throughout the year;
- [ ] employers have their own Web sites – you can check out their recruitment needs, products and services, plus their mission and worldwide locations in minutes!

'What about a training scheme?'

There are a range of training schemes available all over the UK, and careers services will have details. You get relevant experience, training and qualifications (plus cash – not just a training allowance), so check them out. They cover a whole range of careers, so there's bound to be something to suit you – a careers adviser will help you find it. At least you're *inside* the gang of workers, rather than *outside*.

Check:

- [ ] where a training scheme will get you in two, three and five years' time;
- [ ] what qualifications you can get through them;
- [ ] what chances of promotion there might be with the company you're joining;
- [ ] what sort of companies offer apprenticeships and training programmes;
- [ ] by talking to people who are currently trainees on them, preferably in an area you want to work in;
- [ ] what skills and knowledge you'll acquire;
- [ ] how much real responsibility you'll get and how quickly.

Remember that the more you put into work, the more you will get out of it. This applies whatever level you're at.

INCREASE YOUR CHANCES OF GETTING A JOB

When you start applying for jobs, increase your chances of success by following some simple guidelines.

top T I P

If you're applying for a job or a course, remember that *many application forms, letters and CVs go straight in the bin.* Why? Because they are full of spelling mistakes, grammatical errors and tell the employer nothing.

So increase your chances of success.

INFORMATION POINT

Get help and advice from your careers service. They will have information on how to:

- complete an application form;
- write a CV;
- put a letter together to introduce yourself to an employer;
- handle an interview;
- send speculative letters and CVs.

Make use of your careers service and your chances of success will *rocket*.

7 golden rules to follow:

1. Practise doing the application form, writing a letter or doing your CV before doing the 'final' version. Keep a copy of the final version you send off.
2. Double-check your work for spelling and grammatical errors – and then get somebody else to check again for you.
3. Don't send anything off with stains, creases or dirty marks on it – aim for a clean, crisp copy.
4. Don't use flowery paper or stationery with pictures on it – get clean, white A4-sized paper.
5. Think about what the selector – be it an employer or course tutor – wants in any applicant. Try to show you have the right qualities and skills they need.
6. Show you've found something out about the company and the industry or sector you're applying to, especially if you're at university.
7. Use your National Record of Achievement (NRA) and the exercises you've done in this book to help you prepare your application. Take your NRA to the interview with you.

top T I P

Many applicants of all ages don't make the link in their application to show how their strengths, interests, talents and abilities are just what employers want. Be sure you *do*. Your careers adviser can show you how.

Check with your referees that you may put their name down. Tell them what you're applying for.

Some careers services will give you a mock interview so that
you have an opportunity to practise your interview skills. Take
the chance to try this – you'll get some useful feedback.

'Well, we'll get back to you…'

Many employers don't respond to applicants who've applied
for posts advertised in the paper, for all sorts of reasons, so
why not get back to them?

WORK IT OUT

Follow up applications:

1.   Call them up and ask to speak to the person you had
     to contact about the job initially.
2.   Show you're aware that they are busy – appreciate
     the pressure they're probably under.
3.   Ask what happens to your details now – are they kept
     on file?
4.   Check to see if you should call in a few months' time
     to see if they have another vacancy.
5.   Make the call and remind them of your interest.
6.   Keep calling, and do something relevant in the
     meantime.

'I WANT A YEAR OFF OR AT LEAST SOME TIME OUT.'

There is nothing wrong in taking time out if you do something
constructive, ie an activity you can put on a CV or application
form and discuss in an interview. Many people have a year
out to save some money before starting university. Often,
graduates want a last bit of fun before settling down to working
life.

Constructive things to do
Activities you can put on your CV that show you have a 'get-up-and-go' attitude and can talk about at an interview.

Non-constructive things to do
Going to the pub, night clubs; lazing in bed until lunch-time; and watching telly and videos.

The danger of taking a year out is that you don't do anything in it and by the time you've planned what you're going to do, it's practically over.

'You're not taking a year off!'

Many parents dread the idea of you taking time out. It fills them with horror. A year out can be difficult to manage. Think about it: after so many years of being told what to do and spending so much time in education with its timetables, homework, rules and dress code, you suddenly have a free time all day, every day. *Bliss!* Could you handle it? Your parents probably worry you won't.

Most people couldn't handle lots of time out. 'I'd go *mad* if I didn't have anything to do,' they say. One reason people 'enjoy' work is for the friendship and the sense of belonging. Plus, work provides a routine to life, and an income. The people who retire with lots of things lined up to do generally enjoy retirement the most. Why? Because they are busy, active, participating in society and feeling useful. And the same is true of people who've left school, college or university. People need to feel needed and useful, if they are going to live happy and fulfilled lives.

If you've been at university, you might find time out easier to handle – but employers will still want to see what you did in your time out.

 How do *you* handle lots of free time?

To get an idea of what your time management, planning skills and motivation are like, think back to your last summer holidays.

☐ Did you plan anything specific to do on your own? If yes, what?

☐ Did you plan things to do with your friends? If yes, what?

☐ How did you fill your time in the end?

☐ What did you do last summer holidays that you could put down on an application form for a job?

☐ Did you do all the things you set out to do last summer holidays? If yes, why?

☐ If no, why not? Was it because:
  - Summer was too short   _____
  - I couldn't be bothered   _____
  - It's supposed to be my time off to relax!   _____
  - Why should I do anything?   _____
  - I was too busy with course work   _____
  - We had a family holiday – I couldn't fit it all in   _____
  - Never thought of actually *doing* anything   _____

If you easily filled your time with things you could put on a CV, you'll probably handle time out fairly well, because you're used to getting up and doing things for yourself. You're what the workplace would describe as an 'achiever' and a 'do-er' – you get things done.

If you didn't, think twice about taking a year out. If you don't motivate yourself to do something, you'll probably waste a year doing nothing. Then you'll get bored, disillusioned with life, disappointed with yourself and angry at your situation. That's no fun.

top T I P

Employers always want to know what you did in any gaps between jobs, and between education and jobs. They accept there will be some – but they worry about taking people on who do literally nothing.

 Why are you interested in taking a year out?

Here are some reasons why people take a year out. Which one might fit into your long-term goal?

Is this you?

To decide what I want to do	_____
To get some work experience in a field related to my career	_____
Because it's necessary to go on to do the course I want to do	_____
To travel (after I've got some money together by working for about six months)	_____
To do a volunteer programme in the UK/abroad	_____
To work in industry for a year to get some experience	_____
To have a break before I start the long haul of studying I need to do	_____
To go out to work in a full-time job so that I can find out more about the workplace – everybody has to start somewhere	_____
Other (write it down)	_____

6   reasons to plan a year out well before it happens:

1. To check all your options and be able to say, yes, I'm taking the right one.
2. Because some programmes have long application procedures (like 18 months) – you don't want to miss anything.
3. To save money, in case you want to travel, or go on a programme that costs you.
4. To get ahead of everybody else in the search for a job or in the application process.
5. To convince your parents that this is what you want to do.
6. To put down on application forms for uni or employers, if you're applying in advance. *'I'm going to teach English to French school children next year – it's all set up,'* is more convincing than, *'I'm going to have a year off.'*

---

i

INFORMATION POINT

Finding out what you can do in your time out:

- Check with your careers service and job centre for vacancies.
- Visit employment agencies and register before everybody else. Keep in regular contact with them.
- Write to employers directly to see whether they would be willing to take you on for a year. Some companies offer jobs to young people for a year, understanding that you want a year out.

Use it to think about what you want to do: many people come to the end of a year out without having moved their career planning any further forward.

WORK IT OUT

Moving forward:

1. Think about the career you want.
2. Find out what you need to get there.
3. Check out local opportunities to train, study or learn.
4. Match them to your needs and interests.
5. Apply for the course.
6. Apply yourself, ie *work!*

FINAL POINTS

☐ Use any chance you get to develop skills and qualities that employers will want – more on those in the next chapter.

☐ Remember to look ahead to where you want to go – and you're more likely to end up there.

| Q | **Summary Exercises**

The course of action which will help me work in the sector (and job) I want is:

_____

_____

_____

The entry qualifications I'll need to get to my next short-term goal are:

_____

_____

The application method is:

_____

I need to apply by:

_____

What I'll do if I don't get in is:

_____

Building up skills and qualities required at work

This chapter is going to look more generally at the sorts of skills and qualities required in virtually any job. So here goes!

HAVE YOU GOT ATTITUDE?

top T I P

The right attitude is essential if you want to succeed at work.

At any level of work, the right attitude is important. Here are some qualities that help create the right impression – and you can't get qualifications for these. How is your attitude? Go through these below – before you look at the answers, cross-check your thoughts with a friend, relative or teacher.

Put Yes or No	Are/Do You?	Meaning:
_____	Punctual	You turn up on time.
_____	Reliable	You don't ring in sick – you turn up.
_____	Motivated	You get things done, get results and make things happen.
_____	Interested	You're interested in what you're doing and other people.
_____	Work hard	You concentrate on the job on hand to make sure it gets done in time. You work at a consistent pace throughout the day.
_____	Polite	You don't swear, shout or show aggression towards others.
_____	Cheerful	You're a smiling, happy person to have around.
_____	A team player	You ask other people how you can help.
_____	Willing to go the extra mile	You're willing to go the extra mile, ie do something without being asked or expecting any reward.
_____	Flexible	You're willing to adjust your hours, and take on tasks not normally expected of you.

So what's your attitude like?

8–10 Yesses: You've got attitude – and it's in the right place. You'll go far.

5–7 Yesses: Watch your attitude! It gets carried away a bit sometimes – in the wrong direction.

1–4 Yesses: You've got attitude – an attitude problem. If you wanted to be fired, you wouldn't be far off.

PRACTISE KEY SKILLS

Some skills are very important at work and you should try to improve them at every chance you get. Here they are:

☐ **Communication skills** – to set out and present information and ideas, and express yourself clearly. If you're socializing well with your friends, you'll be communicating with them:

  – listening to what they're saying, nodding to say you got the message, saying '*yeah*' at intervals;
  – talking to them in a language you all understand;
  – relating to them;
  – letting everybody have their say.

☐ **Information technology** – to prepare, process and present information in a variety of ways, use the Internet, e-mail, spreadsheets, databases, word processing;

☐ **Numeracy** – to use statistics, graphs, flow charts, spreadsheets;

☐ **Solving problems** – to identify and understand a problem, and then to find a solution;

☐ **Working with others and on your own;**

☐ **Improving your own learning and performance.**

top **T I P**

Keep examples of skills you've used at work so that you can show employers how you use skills. For example, keep a record of problems you've identified and solved to show you have skills in problem solving.

Whatever you do at work, you'll need these key skills to do a good job. So look for chances to work on these skills and to get qualifications in them. Courses are increasingly designed to give students the skills employers want, and so increasing their chances of landing a job.

Fact

The workplace is fast-paced. Technology means that you can respond to requests at the push of a button. Get to grips with IT, and get work experience, so that you can hit the ground running.

WORK IT OUT

Ways to develop your skills:

- At home – as you live with your family, relatives, neighbours, family and friends.
- In full-time education and extra curricular activities.
- Through paid work such as summer jobs, and Saturday work.
- Through hobbies and interests.

You can practise many of these skills at work, on work experience, through participation in training schemes, voluntary work, case studies in class ... for starters! Collect examples of skills you've practised to tell future employers about at interview or in your application.

Even if you're not sure you know what sort of career you want, you can develop a really useful set of skills which can be used in many different sectors.

USING SATURDAY/HOLIDAY JOBS TO FIND OUT MORE

Get a Saturday job or help out in some capacity where you will be meeting people to develop your skills in communicating with people, handling situations, problem solving and customer service.

Look for work, be it paid, unpaid, full-time or part-time, holiday or Saturdays, in sectors which have typically offered lots of this type of work:

Sector	Job
retail	sales assistant, cashier
tourism	waitress, bar work, washing up
commerce/industry	temping
caring sector	babysitting, holiday camp work, working in an OAPs' home, with disabled
customer service	call centre
agriculture/horticulture	soft fruit picking
media	working on student newspaper
computing/IT	inputting data
banking/finance	sales assistant, cashier

Even as a graduate, you can use this sort of work experience to show an employer you've developed skills the company wants.

---

i

INFORMATION POINT

Where can I find details on these sorts of jobs?

Places to try include a book called *Vacation Work* (useful if there is high unemployment in your area), the local press, your job centre, careers office and approaching companies direct.

WORKING IN A TEAM

Working well in a team means you can:

- [ ] work with a group of people to achieve a goal;
- [ ] understand how the team works and the role everyone has to play in it;
- [ ] make friends and contacts;
- [ ] feel satisfied, by achieving a goal as a team.

DO YOU WORK WELL IN A TEAM?

Think of the last time you worked on something with a group of people you didn't know very well, either in or out of school, such as a project, team sport, or musical.

1. How did you cope working with people you didn't know?
2. Did you all pull together quickly to work as a team?
3. Did you all argue a lot?
4. Was there an agreed outcome?
5. Did you meet the deadline?
6. Who was the leader? Was there an obvious leader?
7. What part did you play?

8. How long did it take to start pulling together and feel as though you were getting somewhere as a team?
9. Did you all have the same goal?
10. Did you all listen to what each other had to say? Or did some people get to do all the talking? How did that make everybody else in the team feel?

---

i

INFORMATION POINT

Ways to develop your team-working skills include:

■ taking part in team sports;
■ theatrical productions;
■ musical groups – orchestras, bands, choirs;
■ community service organizations and activities;
■ adventure activities;
■ work experience;
■ voluntary work.

DEVELOP A COMPETITIVE SPIRIT

Britain's businesses and organizations have to be lean, mean fighting units to survive the competitive jungle that's life in today's workplace.

Most areas of life are competitive now. Look at league tables for schools and universities. When you get ahead of the pack, you have to make sure that that's where you're going to stay.

Challenge Yourself!

Put yourself in competitive situations.
Get used to competing – you'll be doing it a lot in your working life.

You might compete as an individual or a company:

☐ for that job against other people;
☐ for a contract of work, perhaps working for a company;
☐ as a self-employed person, for a slice of the market;
☐ against other businesses in your sector;
☐ against international companies.

WORK IT OUT

Develop your competitive spirit!

■ Get practice in handling competitive situations or proving yourself.
■ Get used to preparing yourself for the big event.
■ Learn what it's like to be in a competitive situation, up against other people.
■ Feel that need to win, to come first, to be the first choice, to be the winner.
■ Remember that feeling. Aim to repeat it in your work.

Competing in different events will help you identify your strengths (compared with other people's), and explain to selectors the standard you've reached: '*In the recent speed test we did in our keyboard lesson, I got 47 words per minute*'; or, '*I have a good memory – I used to get over 80 per cent in our vocab tests in French.*' If you can give a figure or fact to show your strength, it will always mean more than saying, *'I can type quickly'* or *'I remember things well.'*

Here are some examples of competitive situations:

□   going for a role you want in a play;
□   entering a competition;
□   applying for a part-time job;
□   applying for a place on a course;
□   doing an exam of any sort, eg music, dance, first aid – anything that measures your performance;
□   standing for election to a committee;
□   taking part in sport.

Fact

The world is more competitive	– firms are competing for business locally, nationally and internationally. Know how a business functions, who is responsible for what, and how to spot opportunities.
It's international	– the smallest firm can do business worldwide thanks to the Internet. Knowing how to use the Internet to market services and products will be useful.

Work experience and reading the business pages of newspapers will help to sharpen your awareness of how organizations work and compete for business.

 How much do you care about doing something well?

□   Do you always do the very best you can?
   –   In the way you behave towards others?

- In competitions?
- In any activity you take part in?
☐ Do you take pride in your work?
☐ Are you proud of your school, college or university?
☐ Are you proud of what you've achieved so far in your life?

The will to do your best is very important at work.

CAN YOU HANDLE CHANGE?

Okay, so the only thing we can be sure of today is that things are changing. Fast. Knowledge today is history tomorrow. Employees and organizations have to keep on top of all sorts of change, including new laws that affect them (from both the UK and Europe), mergers with other companies, new technology, and generally just new ways of doing things which can make them better, faster, cheaper and more successful than the next guy. So you have to be able to cope with things coming at you at a fast pace, while still handling your day-to-day routine stuff. This is one of the reasons why it's important to be flexible and keep learning.

ARE YOU WILLING TO KEEP LEARNING?

'Well, why should qualifications matter?'
  Qualifications prove you can:

☐ learn and continue to learn – employers will be able to teach you how to do the work they want you to do. *You'll be able to master new technology.*
☐ stick with it – you won't give up when the work gets more difficult. *You'll just get on with it and persist.*

- ☐ succeed – your exam results are the first proof an employer has that you can succeed. *It's going to be worth training you.*
- ☐ reach a certain standard. *Your prospective employer knows that you have 54 words per minute.*

Qualifications are more important to some employers than others. For example, accountancy and legal firms will look more closely at your GCSE and A level or GNVQ results than other employers, especially if you are intending to take up a career for which further study and training are required (which the employer will be paying for). But throughout the UK, there will be special training programmes for people who left school early without any qualifications. Careers services will have details of these.

WHY IS IT SO IMPORTANT TO KEEP LEARNING?

Answer TRUE or FALSE, depending on your point of view!

The world is changing more rapidly than ever before. _____
Knowledge goes out of date very quickly. _____
It is important to keep up to date with new
techniques and research if you are to do your job
properly and well. _____
Even when you are older, you should keep learning
(if only to keep up with your grandchildren!). _____
If you're in a job just for the sake of it, you shouldn't
waste your time learning at night. It won't lead
anywhere. _____
When I finish doing full-time education, I shan't
have to bother learning or studying anymore if I
don't want to. _____
There are more ways to train for things now than
there ever have been before. _____

Now talk to people at work, or discuss your answers with your mates. What would their answers be?

Some methods of training may be new to you:

☐ **Day release**   one day a week at college, released from your workplace to learn, study or train;

☐ **Block release**   you spend a block of time studying for something, eg two or three weeks;

☐ **Mentoring**   somebody is your mentor, who helps you develop your career. You might meet with them from time to time, or sit alongside them as they work;

☐ **Evening class**   you go to college one evening a week to work for a qualification;

☐ **On the job**   somebody shows you how to do something. Usually they have been doing the work for some time.

Professional and vocational qualifications that you work for show employers and customers that you:

☐ have met a specified standard of knowledge and skills;

☐ have the skills you need;

☐ have proof that you are genuinely interested in doing the best job you can by keeping up to date with changes in the sector;

☐ have met certain compulsory subjects (ie 'if you don't study mathematics, there's no way you can be an architect');

☐ want to progress.

FINAL POINTS

☐ Be prepared to keep learning at any level – it's the best way to make sure you'll always have a job.

☐ Have the right attitude and show customers that you really care about them and you'll go far.

Q **Summary Exercises**

☐ Describe something you've done that you're really, really pleased about. What did it involve? Why were you so pleased about it?

☐ Describe a major change you've had in your life. How did you handle it?

CHAPTER NINE

Dealing with feelings, fears and concerns

'I might fail!'

Some people put off doing things because they fear they might fail. Don't let this happen to you. Just do your research and find out as much as you can about the sector you want to work in. The more you do, the less likely you are to make the wrong decision. For starters, it always impresses employers and course selectors when you can talk about the sector you're going to work in, and show an interest in it. So what else can you do?

top T I P

Boost your skills and experience. You'll increase your chances of getting a job.

Can you think of something extra to offer that very few people applying for a job would have? In some jobs, it's useful to have skills like:

- ☐ a heavy goods vehicle licence;
- ☐ a driving licence;
- ☐ a first aid certificate;
- ☐ the ability to speak in public;
- ☐ the ability to speak a foreign language;
- ☐ shorthand skills.

You can get some of these courses at night school, or by studying them privately.

'I'll get laughed at!'

If your friends laugh at you when you say you're thinking of being a whatever, then they might be:

- ☐ jealous – you've thought of something and they can't think of anything;
- ☐ nervous – what should they say?
- ☐ not your friends.

So ignore them.

Professional people won't laugh when you talk about your career options. They'll be pleased you're doing something about it. Show a professional approach by taking yourself and your career seriously. Share your thoughts with them. Get their advice. Listen to it and learn from it.

'I couldn't! I'm far too shy! Please don't make me!'

It's often awkward when you're meeting people for the first time, especially if it's on work experience or in an interview situation. Shyness is a problem for people of all ages. The man running a business may be at a complete loss at a dinner party. You may find it very difficult to get to talk to people without blushing, trembling, and wishing the earth would open up and swallow you up, so...

Challenge Yourself!

Practise putting yourself into situations where you will have to meet and talk to people you don't know. You'll communicate with older people at work. *Practise* communicating with people outside your age group.

Talk to the elderly lady at the bus stop, the person on checkout ... it doesn't matter who they are. *Practise* talking to people. Talk about the weather, their dog, garden or car ... *anything* that starts up a conversation. And if you do suffer from shyness, get a job where you *have* to meet people – a shop or supermarket.

'My family are no help at all. They're just not interested.'

If you feel that your family don't care about you, please don't suffer alone. There are plenty of people who will give you the help you need to think about your future, from your local careers officer, to a favourite teacher or perhaps a friend's mum or dad. Let them know how you're doing and keep in close contact with them. Talk to friends about their career plans and share your thoughts and fears. You can bet many of your year will be feeling slightly nervous about leaving education and heading off, free for the first time. Tell your mum or dad how you're feeling and ask them for some help and support – they aren't mind-readers, and may not know what you're going through.

'I'm always arguing with mum or dad. They're so stressed out all the time. Why can't they just chill out?'

Gaining your independence is a difficult time for you and your parents. Your parents have worries of their own, like:

☐ letting you go as they get older;
☐ wishing they had the opportunities you now have when they were your age;
☐ helping you through the whole child to adult process – are they doing a good job and giving you the right sort of support?
☐ finding the right balance between showing you they care, laying down the law and letting you live your life.

Plus they'll also be thinking about their careers, tax bills, pensions, elderly relatives and their own body changes – the middle-age bulge and droop, lines and the menopause (mostly women) and baldness (men).

top T I P

Your parents will still refer to you as their child when you're 60 and they're 80. Don't waste your time and energy trying to persuade them otherwise.

'What job? No chance where I live – nobody I know is working. I'm headed for a life in front of the telly and hanging round the streets.'

If there are high unemployment rates in your home town, plan an escape route out.

 ways to escape unemployment:

1. Go through college, get work experience, join a training scheme. Your careers service will help you. Let an education be your tunnel out.
2. If you want to stay in your home town, ask your careers service which avenues of employment are *expanding*. Get training and a job in those areas. It's easier to move from work to work than unemployment to work. And find out what effect the Internet is having on job opportunities in your area.
3. Think about doing temporary jobs as a way to get into organizations. Many people make a career out of doing this – they can work when it suits them!
4. Join a voluntary programme that offers you food and somewhere to live, like CSV (see 'Useful Addresses').
5. If you have relatives who are living in an area where employment rates are higher, see if you can stay with them for a while.

Challenge Yourself!

Don't spend the day watching telly, even if other members of your family do. Get out and be different.

Fill your time with things that will increase your chances of being offered a job.

'What is there to do, though?'

☐ Get involved in a charity – pick up skills working in a retail shop, selling a magazine, organizing a jumble sale.

☐ Offer to do odd jobs – washing cars, mowing lawns, feeding pets, baby-sitting.

☐ Learn new skills through voluntary work or college courses. Study IT, languages, customer service courses. There are usually discounts for people who are unemployed.

☐ Join a training programme and get work experience you can put on your CV.

☐ Keep fit – doing something physical will help you ward off feelings of aggression and anger.

INFORMATION POINT

Keeping busy when you're unemployed:

Call your local youth service who'll have a number of activities set up in the area and who'll put you in touch with local organizations which can help. Plus there's your local Citizens' Advice Bureau – their number is in the Yellow Pages.

top T I P

If people see you are trying to help yourself, they will help you. Act smart, not stupid.

Remember the resources on offer to you. Go back to page 25 in Chapter 2 and remind yourself what they are. Talk to your careers service about the benefits which might apply. Check what you need to do to receive them, though, because you might have to enrol for a short programme to help you prepare for work or improve your job-hunting skills, while you're waiting for the right opportunity to come your way. Visit them regularly, so they know you're trying your best to get work. You have to show willing.

'I want to invest in my future. How?'

There are two sorts of investments you can make: savings and training.

top T I P

When you are getting paid for work you do, try to save a set amount of money. Stick it into a savings account. That money will be really useful, one day.

INFORMATION POINT

Get literature from banks and building societies about their products:

Banks and building societies regard you as a customer with potential. They know that one day you'll get a job and earn money. Visit your local banks and building societies to find out which has the best products for you – they'll have plenty of product literature advertising their wares and you can talk to an adviser too.

top T I P

A problem for many relatives is what to get you for Christmas/birthdays. Why not ask them to put money into your savings accounts? You solve their problem of what to get you – and save them time.

The second major investment you can make is in training. The workplace is such that not every employer can offer training, despite initial promises made at interview:

'We're firm believers in training, of course...'

Many employers offer new staff training programmes but then they don't happen. Staff don't have the time to set them up, an important project means that training gets forgotten, that deadline means you'll have to miss your weekly stint at college. They don't do it deliberately. Wise employees invest in their future themselves, rather than leaving it all to their employers.

WORK IT OUT

Invest in your future:

- Know where you want to be in five years' time – and plan your own training needs to get you there.
- Know what training is on offer locally.
- Train and study in your spare time.

Planning your own training programme means you can develop skills that will be useful for other companies, as well as your present employer. It will strengthen your chances of being in work.

 Summary Exercises

Challenge Yourself!

Record everything you do that you achieve and feel proud of.

WHY?

1. When you feel low, look through your diary and boost your confidence.
2. It will remind you of what you do really well and what you enjoy.
3. It will be something to talk about on an application form, in an interview or at a chance meeting with an employer – *show* them you have pride in your work.

CHAPTER TEN

Moving on

SO WHERE ARE WE?

Let's look at what this book has covered and where you are.

In Chapter	You
1	Decided whether you want to force the pace of your career, or just drift.
2	Looked at the different sectors. Found out where you could go for information and advice. Developed strategies for coping with the pains and hassles in your life.
3	Looked at your hobbies, interests, talents, skills and strengths. Worked out which ones you'd like to use in future. Decided what role IT will play in your future career.
4	Worked out what success means to you and what's important to you in life. Decided how far you want to go and assessed if you've got what it takes to get there.
5	Looked at the sort of day-to-day work you want.

In Chapter	You
6	Looked in more detail at job sectors and careers themselves. Continued your research and got first-hand knowledge.
7	Worked out where you need to go from here – sat down with a careers adviser and decided whether to stay in education or go out to work, or take time out (not off!).
8	Looked at ways to boost skills which will help you in the workplace.
9	Developed strategies for handling problems, like unemployment.
10	Here we are!

GOT A PROBLEM AND WANT TO TALK ABOUT IT?

There's nothing wrong in asking for help. A small problem is easier to solve than a big one. And there are people who can help you, you know – you don't have to face things on your own. A confidential chat with them will help you start to sort things out. Some of the following may be of help – their numbers will be in the Yellow Pages, or you can get more information from your local Citizens' Advice Bureau, the library and the Internet.

Your careers service will put you in touch with people who'll help you solve a host of problems – finding somewhere to live, things to do to meet people, difficulties with your partner.

One thing you *won't* avoid at work is handling difficult colleagues. Stay calm, keep your temper, take deep breaths and work to prove them wrong. Don't leave just because they're there. If they're bullying you, record every incident and report the member of staff to the boss or personnel. You have rights, you know.

WORK IT OUT

Get help when things aren't going well and talk to:

- careers advisers at college/university or your local careers service;
- student counsellors;
- your GP;
- the family planning clinic;
- your bank/building society;
- your supervisor, the boss, a colleague you trust;
- mum or dad;
- a friend who's just started work recently too – maybe they're having similar problems.

HAVING ANOTHER CHANCE...

Employers aren't old fossils; they know it's not easy to decide on a career. Some take on graduates with one or two years' work experience, who feel they're not going places fast enough. Others appreciate that it's possible to stray on to the wrong track, like Guy:

> I joined a building society after I left school, but hated it. A careers adviser helped me look at my skills and interests. I joined a training scheme for hotel management – I got paid, got experience and qualifications before moving on to my first job in London. I want to go to Australia next year – get some experience out there, do some surfing... Can't wait.

DON'T STAY AT HOME TOO LONG

Get used to moving for a job – it will help you in the future. You'll be practised in looking for work in areas where there is some.

People who move away to go to university are often more successful finding a job than those who stay at home. Why? Because they have:

☐ had practice in building a life elsewhere;
☐ gained more confidence in their abilities to cope with completely new situations;
☐ become more open-minded to the idea of moving to benefit from opportunities.

Leaving home teaches you to be independent. You'll learn what it's like to find your own place to live, to handle bills, to live with other people, to cope with tax, to deal with the unexpected, like leaking pipes and blocked loos... It will also teach you how to find work in a town other than your own – useful if unemployment is high in your area.

STARTING WORK (OR DOING A STINT OF WORK EXPERIENCE)

In any new job, there's tons to learn, like:

☐ the names of your colleagues, the bosses and customers;
☐ company procedures and processes, like the way things are done;
☐ the job in hand;
☐ your way about;
☐ using the company's IT systems;
☐ what is acceptable and what's not, eg dress and language;
☐ health and safety regulations, eg non-smoking policies – most firms have them;
☐ the company's direction and the part you'll play in its success.

When you're starting your first job, you'll need to organize your life and your work, a bit like you did (or didn't) when you were in full-time education. This includes:

- getting up in time;
- attending to personal hygiene (applying shampoo, soap, deodorant, toothpaste, toothbrush to your body) – there's nothing worse than working with someone with BO and BB (body odour and bad breath);
- getting to work on time;
- deciding what you're going to do for lunch;
- getting home again;
- deciding how to spend your cash after you've paid rent (if you live at home, get into the practice of paying rent to your parents);
- starting out at the bottom – when you left school/college, you were at the top.

Try to balance work, rest and fun. Look at how you're spending your week and prioritize what's essential; can you forget the rest?

Challenge Yourself!

Make an impact!

What is expected of you, the new worker/student	So – do better than that
□ to turn up on time every day	turn up 10 to 15 minutes early every day to get organized

What is expected of you, the new worker/student	So – do better than that
☐ be reliable and willing to do the lower-level tasks – we all have to start somewhere	do what you're asked to do as well as you can
☐ to be enthusiastic and interested in what you are doing	ask questions about the work you're given and what the section's doing: show an interest
☐ don't hit the door at 5.00 pm	stay until your work is done
☐ be cheerful	get to know people; join in as much as you can – a drink after work, going to the café or canteen for lunch
☐ be accurate	double-check your work before you hand it back or show it to your boss
☐ remember all jobs have their dull routine bit	accept them cheerfully. Even the boss has to do the boring stuff.

LOOKING AHEAD

Any number of things might happen to you at work. You might be in line for:

☐ promotion – moving on up;
☐ demotion – moving back down;
☐ sideways move – moving across perhaps to acquire new skills;
☐ being made redundant – 'sorry, we're re-structuring'; or 'sorry, we're letting you go – we just haven't got enough business coming in';
☐ 'you're fired' – unlikely;
☐ work abroad – usually in large professional organizations – 'How would you like to spend two years in New York? You would? Great. Can you start on Monday?'

You must, always, look after number one – you.

> My employers made me redundant after I'd done five years with them. I was devastated, but they gave me a good package and so I travelled for six months. When I got back, I met someone from the company and they said, what was I doing and could I do a few hours a week for them? I did but I charged them about three times an hour what I was earning from them before.
>
> Lauren

People aren't staying in the same place for very long by their own choice – even those at the top

There are now fewer layers of managers in most organizations, so more people are likely to leave to find a new challenge – companies can't promote everyone. Many executives have their details on the register of executive search companies, hoping one day they might get that magic phone call which means they're wanted elsewhere. Bosses are as likely to move on as anyone else, as new opportunities come their way. 'Oh, I love a new challenge,' the boss smiles. (Yesterday, he bawled out a junior manager who was giving his notice in to move on to the competition – 'Where's your loyalty?') Be prepared to leave your company to move on.

6 key skills to surviving in the job market:

1. Know what you're good at and enjoy.
2. Have a strong network of contacts – people who'll always be willing to help you.
3. Know how to apply for a job and how to network.
4. Know how to learn new skills.
5. Be flexible – don't stick rigidly to the tasks listed in your job description.
6. Be prepared to change direction and say 'it's time to move on'.

KEEP DOING THE EXERCISES IN THIS BOOK

They will help you watch your long-term goals and boost your chances of achieving them, if you can. This means visiting notice boards and careers services and checking the local papers regularly to see if there might just be that notice which tells you about a chance to: try something new, do an IT programme, be a volunteer, do a term abroad.

top T I P

Review your long-term goals and keep doing the exercises in this book. People do change their minds and ideals. If this happens to you, be flexible. Use what you've done to provide a basis for your future.

Long-term goals can be shot out of the water by the most unexpected events, throwing your life upside down.

ALL SORTS OF THINGS CAN CHANGE YOUR LIFE IN A FEW MOMENTS...

☐ You meet your future partner. *'Wow...'* And your life is never the same.
☐ You get pregnant, or you get somebody else pregnant. Parenthood is on the way, and you've got yourself a job for life.
☐ You get a chance to travel with work, either to live abroad or to travel on the job.

☐ You get a phone call from a headhunter: 'We've got a job that might interest you...'

☐ You're made redundant. *'What next?'*

☐ Pressure of work makes you think: *'There must be more to life than this ... I've got to get a better balance between work and home.'*

☐ New career opportunities spring up in your area ... a competitor opens up.

☐ Suggestions from friends. 'What we need in this area is a new ... And you'd be absolutely right to set it up, go on your own, start your own business.'

☐ You have chance meetings with prospective new employers.

☐ You get the feeling, *'I'd love to do something different ... I wonder what?'*

☐ Your relatives and their health. *'My mother isn't well. We need to sort out some care for her. I may need to work more from home for a few months, to keep an eye on her.'*

top TIP

Life is an adventure. Few of us really know what lies ahead. That's why the ability to cope with change is really important.

Life is driven by change. It's the only constant factor at work and at home in the 21st century. You can change your life yourself and be in the driving seat by making your own decisions and knowing where you want to go. Much depends on what you want and your attitude to life and your ability to cope with change. The good news is that career paths are more diverse, there are more routes in for the returner, the late developer, the person changing career. So don't be afraid to change career – *expect* to change career. You're not typecast to one job for eternity.

Summary Exercises

These exercises are designed to help you build up enthusiasm and fire for your long-term goal.

Are you:

Up to date with everything that's happening in the sector you want to work in? _____

Reading magazines and newspaper articles relating to it? _____

Talking to people working in it? _____

Looking at the papers for jobs in it? _____

Developing the skills and knowledge you'll need to work in it? _____

Building up a base of examples to show employers that you have the qualities you'll need to do a good job? _____

Feeling as though you're going somewhere with your life? _____

Updating your CV every six months? _____

Going to all the careers events you can to make up a network of contacts from organizations which are in your sector? _____

Making a note of these contacts when you get home in a file? _____

Still meddling/fiddling with your favourite interests and hobbies? _____

Listing the things you feel strongly about: are they still the same or are you taking up new interests which might provide a career? _____

 one final top **T I P**

There aren't really many rules any more about careers. You pave your own path. The world's your oyster. Good luck!

Glossary

A levels/AS levels   Academic qualifications, eg in history, geography, biology. Incorporate Key Skills. Some courses may be compulsory for university training. Can be combined with GNVQs and range of qualifications in post-16 education. Currently being re-structured.

careers interview   Your 30 minutes with a trained, impartial careers adviser who will help you explore your career ideas and update you on the workplace.

ECCTIS 2000   A computer-aided system which will help you find the right course for you and has lots of information about careers.

extra-curricular activities   Anything you do outside of the classroom or lecture hall.

global organization   Company which has offices worldwide. Usually professional companies, eg accountants, banks, lawyers, airlines.

GNVQ   General National Vocational Qualification, three levels, normally one or two years long. Cover wide variety of broad-based sectors, giving introduction to each, eg business studies, information technology, engineering. Offer you the chance to get key skills.

late developers   People who decide what they want to be, or develop their brains, much later than most people – like in their 20s!

mature student   The term 'mature student' is used to classify all students over the age of 21.

NVQ   National Vocational Qualification. A qualification you acquire by being assessed on what you can do (and have learnt) in the workplace. Five levels, one (lowest) to five (highest).

professional bodies   Organizations that set out the ethics and standards expected of their members.

professional exams   The exams laid out by a sector or industry's professional body to ensure certain standards are met.

skills   Things you can *do*, not necessarily at work.

SMEs   Small- and medium-sized companies. They form an important part of the economy and should not be forgotten in your search for a job.

supporters   People who'll cheer you on and who you can talk to about your career.

vocational courses   Courses relating to a career or sector, eg art and design, photography, information technology.

voluntary work   Unpaid efforts, usually to help others less fortunate than you. Can be very useful way to boost your skills and get into the workplace.

Further reading

Your careers library and the Internet have a *huge* amount of information ready for you to browse through at your leisure. Keep them busy – that's what they're there for. Here are some books you might find particularly useful.

INFORMATION ON SPECIFIC CAREERS

Alexander, L (1996) *Finding a Job with a Future*, How to Books
Sharma, S (2000) *The Times A–Z of Careers and Jobs*, 9th edn, Kogan Page, London
Careers in ... series by Kogan Page, London, giving an excellent insight into different careers.
Casebooks, covering a range of subjects, are a series published by Hobsons containing lots of information and case studies.
Great Careers for People Interested in... series by Kogan Page, London, available in your careers library or bookshops.
Long, J (1997) *Great Careers for People Interested in Being an Entrepreneur*, Kogan Page, London
Occupations, published annually by COIC and available in careers services and public libraries. A mine of information!

STAYING ON IN EDUCATION

Financial Help in Further Education, produced by the Department for Employment and Education. Copies are available free from your local careers service or public library.

Financial Support for Students, produced by the Department for Employment and Education for students going on to higher education. Copies available from your local careers service and public library.

Sponsorship for Students, Hobsons Publishing

The University and College Entrance Guide: The Official Guide (annual), available from bookshops and careers libraries. Lists all the courses available and the sorts of qualifications you need to get in.

GETTING WORK TO BOOST YOUR SKILLS

Hempshell, M (1998) *Planning Your Gap Year*, How To Books Ltd

Longson, S (1999) *Making Work Experience Count*, How To Books Ltd – how to get work experience related to your career plans and make the most of it

Summer Jobs, Vacation Work (or visit their Web site on www.vacationwork.co.uk)

APPLYING FOR JOBS

Greenwood, D (1999) *The Job Hunter's Handbook*, Kogan Page, London

GET 2000, published by Hobsons Publishing annually. Lists thousands of vacancies available for graduates, plus hot tips on finding work and applying for jobs. Visit their Web site at www.get.hobsons.co.uk.

Hitchin, P (1996) *Getting your First Job*, How To Books Ltd

Johnstone, J (1997) *Applying for a Job*, How To Books Ltd

McGee, P (1997) *Writing a CV that Works*, How to Books Ltd

Useful addresses

EDUCATION

Careers and Occupational Information Centre (COIC), Moorfoot, Sheffield S1 4PQ (tel: 0114 259 4564)

EDEXCEL, Stewart House, 32 Russell Square, London WC1B 5DN (tel: 0207 413 8400). Will send information on BTEC courses and GNVQs approved by them.

OCR Examinations Board, Westwood Way, Coventry CV4 8JQ (tel: 01203 470033). Will send out information on RSA courses.

UCAS, Rosehill, New Barn Lane, Cheltenham, Gloucester GL51 3LZ (tel: 01242 227788 (general enquiries)). The Universities and Colleges Admissions Service. For details on university courses, visit their Web site: http://www.ucas.ac.uk

www.prospects.csu.ac.uk – contains information on postgraduate courses.

HELP!

The Commission for Racial Equality, Elliot House, 10–12 Allington Street, London SW1E 5EH (tel: 0207 828 7022)

Equal Opportunities Commission, Overseas House, Quay Street, Manchester M3 3HN (tel: 0161 838 8242 for Customer Contact Point)

SKILL, 4th Floor, Chapter House, 18–20 Crucifix Lane, London SW1 3JW. Help for disabled students.

GETTING WORK EXPERIENCE

BUNAC (British Universities North America Club), 16 Bowling Green Lane, London EC1R 0QH (tel: 0207 251 3472)

Community Service Volunteers (CSV), 237 Pentonville Road, London N1 9NJ (tel: 0207 278 6601)

GAP Activity Projects, overseas work for those seeking a year out: 44 Queen's Road, Reading, Berkshire RG1 4BB (tel: 0118 959 4914)

Shell Technology Enterprise Programme (STEP), 11 St Bride Street, London EC4A 4AS (tel: 0207 547 3556)

www.prospects.csu.ac.uk has details of work experience placements for university students.

The Year in Industry, Simon Building, University of Manchester, Oxford Road, Manchester M13 9PL (tel: 0161 275 2000)

SETTING UP YOUR OWN BUSINESS

British Franchise Association, Thames View, Newton Road, Henley on Thames, Oxon RG9 1HG (tel: 01491 578049)

The Prince's Trust. Contact your local careers service for your nearest contact point.

MONEY

Career Development Loans (tel: 0800 585 505, Monday to Friday, 8.00 am–10.00 pm)

Department of Education, Student Support Branch, Rathgael House, Balloo Road, Bangor, County Down BT19 7PR (tel: 01247 279000)

Students Awards Agency for Scotland, Gyleview House, 3 Redheughs Rigg, South Gyle, Edinburgh EH12 9HH (tel: 0131 476 8212)

Student Loans Company Ltd, 100 Bothwell Street, Glasgow G2 7GD

Index